THE FAITH ETERNAL
AND
THE MAN OF TODAY

THE FAITH ETERNAL
AND
THE MAN OF TODAY

by
Jean Cardinal Danielou

translated by
PAUL JOSEPH OLIGNY

FRANCISCAN HERALD PRESS

THE FAITH ETERNAL AND THE MAN OF TODAY, by Jean Cardinal Danielou, translated by Paul Joseph Oligny. Copyright ©1970 by Franciscan Herald Press, 1434 West 51st Street, Chicago, Illinois 60609. Library of Congress Catalog Card Number: 78-123596; ISBN 8199-0407-4. Made in the United States of America.

NIHIL OBSTAT:
  Augustine Rock, O.P.
  Censor Deputatus

IMPRIMATUR:
  Rt. Rev. Msgr. Francis W. Byrne
  Vicar General, Archdiocese of Chicago

June 2, 1970

"The Nihil Obstat and the Imprimatur are official declarations that a book or pamphlet is free of doctrinal or moral error. No implication is contained therein that those who have granted the Nihil Obstat and Imprimatur agree with the contents, opinions, or statements expressed."

Introduction

Christians today feel that they are being questioned about their faith on all sides. Parents are being questioned by their children, students by their comrades, and priests by the laity.

This merciless questioning makes them conscious of all that is unauthentic in their Christianity: sociological conformisms, moral compromises, and doctrinal superficiality. But at the same time it obliges them, if they wish to accept the challenge hurled at them, to lay bare the foundations of their faith.

It is this situation that gave birth to this book. In substance it was first delivered in the form of conferences organized by the Equipes Notre-Dame for Christian lay persons who were seeking to rediscover the bases of their Christianity.

This book therefore, is an attempt to answer fundamental questions concerning belief in God, the transcendence of Christianity as opposed to other religions, the foundation and content of faith in Christ, and finally questions concerning the development of faith in theology and mysticism.

Two attitudes are possible in this present-day questioning. For some, it begins with calling the faith itself into question and goes beyond the inadequacies of believers; for others, it is a source of renewal in that it makes greater demands on their thinking and living. It remains to be shown that this second way is the only way in which, it is hoped, this little book will be helpful.

Contents

Introduction	v
I. The Religious Crisis in the Modern World	3
II. The Foundations of our Belief in God	25
III. Natural Religion — Christian Revelation	43
IV. The Content of Faith	65
V. The Foundations of Faith	83
VI. The Growth of Faith	101

THE FAITH ETERNAL
AND
THE MAN OF TODAY

I: The Religious Crisis In the Modern World

The basic question men of today are asking is not so much concerned with knowing how a little more technical progress can assure man's increasing mastery over the world: this mastery is moving at a pace that fills us with admiration. But the problem troubling men today is to decide what particular notion of man is applicable to the vast resources of today's world; that is the question. In short, the problem consists in knowing what man is, for only to the extent that we know what man is can we have points of reference in order to know how to guide the civilization now in the process of being built on the material plane — a civilization which, if it does not have a corresponding spiritual dimension, can certainly become a hell. And we must admit that today we are getting at the very root of the question. We feel that vague humanisms, vague altruisms, vague personalisms cannot provide the answer; today we know that everything depends on the position we take regarding the problem of God.

It is in terms of the problem of God, and around this problem, that the two great families of minds confront each other: those who think that there is an authentic humanism only in the avowal of God, and those who think that there is an authentic humanism only in the negation of God. The very foundation of atheism is the affirmation that man becomes an adult only on the day he takes upon himself alone the future of his destiny, and from that day on no longer looks to anyone else for help or assistance. This argument of atheism is subtly corrosive for a great number of young people. Now, our position is that there is no humanism outside of God. We refuse to call a godless humanism humanism, because for us a humanism without God is a humanism that deprives man of a part of himself. We respect atheists; we do not respect atheism, because to us atheism seems to be a mutilation inflicted on man. That is why we are embarrassed by the inferiority complexes and the susceptibilities which too many present-day Christians exhibit when confronted with atheism — as if they were somewhat ashamed of being Christians, as if the fact of believing in God could be regarded as the expression of some kind of undefinable, cultural survival, as if the religious animal were an animal destined soon to disappear, and as if they felt that they were the last representatives of a species in the process of extinction. It is all too clear that, considered in this way, faith in God is not in the least exciting and that we should not be surprised if the youth of tomorrow desert a church that does no more than defend rear-guard positions.

Our own position is exactly the opposite. We believe that the future of technical civilization will be a religious future. We believe that only a religious humanism will make a great civilization of the civilization of tomorrow; we do not believe that science discredits religion; we believe just the opposite, namely, that the more man develops himself, the more he will recognize the primacy of transcendence. With this in mind, we shall approach this book with the thought that what we must do is precisely to re-awaken that spirit of Christianity which is conscious of its fundamental solidity, prepared to meet the challenges of tomorrow's world, and certain that in the end it holds the promises of the future. And with a Christianity such as that, it will not be difficult to involve a youth that is generous but led astray by bad teachers.

The problem is not that the youth of today are not equally as good as the young people of yesterday. The problem is that we do not know how to give these young people a living and conquering faith to spark them with enthusiasm. Neverthless we feel, and this is our hope, that something is about to be born. What is again being born at this moment is that vital resurgence in the heart of the Christian people which, laying aside all partisan Christianities, whether of the left or of the right, is aimed simply at affirming the integrity of the faith. It is the desire of Christians who refuse to stand by and watch the bases of their faith in God, of their confidence in the Church, and of their love of the sovereign Pontiff be demolished. This is more important than the assembly of contesting priests: this, as I see it, is the outstanding problem today. And we are witnessing its spread. Something is welling up deep within the Christian people; it is not coming from small intellectual groups, of whatever stripe. It is coming instead from the immense mass of those who have kept silent until now but who today are speaking out. It has been said that the issue of this year was speaking up: yes, it was. We were told to take the floor. Well, we shall take it, and we shall take it to express what is on our mind, that is, our desire that this faith which we have received and which we know holds the promises of the future be preserved for us in its integrity and in its plentitude.

I shall devote this book essentially to the bases of our faith. I shall not go into detail regarding its dogmas. As a matter of fact, that is the true problem today. When we ask many Christians their reason for believing, we find that most of them can give none. They are Christians because they were born into Christian families, because they retain an emotional attachment to Christianity, but it is obvious that these reasons do not go very far. The work laid out for us will be to find out what the foundations of our faith are, that is, what enables us to embrace our faith intellectually, in its entirety, in all its clarity, and in all certitude, in the face of the open defiance of the great currents which we meet in the world of today. As long as we are not able to do that, as long as we are not able to justify our reasons for believing in a valid and cogent way to a colleague, a comrade, or an atheist friend, there is a malaise in us. We are quite convinced that what we believe is true, but we find ourselves somewhat wanting when it comes to giving a satisfactory reason for our conviction. And so, we even ask ourselves sometimes about the foundation on which our faith rests. Our faith, indeed, rests on solid bases, but these bases must be clearly stated, and it is this task that we shall undertake together.

This work will deal with two great orders of questions which correspond to the two great aspects of what is so questioned today. One is the problem of God as such, because, as a matter of fact, what is called into question today is essentially this problem. Is God about to disappear in our day and are those who believe in God the representatives of a vanishing race? Are we headed for a post-religious world, that is to say, must we today attempt to learn what Christianity can become in a world where God will no longer be? Or do we, on the contrary, believe that relationship with God is just as basic today to human nature as it was yesterday and that it is only to the extent to which he opens himself to God in his innermost self that man is fully a man?

Next, we shall tackle the problems that more directly relate to faith in Jesus Christ. For, after all, one need not be a Christian to believe that there is a God; there are billions of men, Moslems, Jews, Buddhists, Hindus, and others who, down deep within themselves, believe in God, but still do not accept the Christian faith, the Trinity, the Incarnation, the resurrection, or the outpouring of the Holy Spirit on Pentecost. Here we are in the presence of a second category of questions that go back to different bases. Here we want to know what is the basis of our right to believe with full certitude and not as if our belief were a carry-over from an outdated cultural world. We seek the basis for believing that Christ, the new Adam, was conceived of the Virgin Mary by the Holy Spirit; that by the power of the Spirit he snatched his human body from death and transfigured it at the resurrection. It is obvious that these are events that rest on bases of belief, but on bases different from those that justify belief in the existence of God.

It is, therefore, this fundamental problem of God, of the religious dimension of man, that we must grapple with first. I shall approach it, first of all, by pointing out the questions that are raised. Then, we shall answer these questions by a very simple, but hard and fast exercise of our intellectual faculty. There is clearly a crisis over the awareness of God in the modern world, a religious crisis. It is important that we try to see what this crisis over the awareness of God corresponds to, because only insofar as we can locate its roots can we supply the correct answers and remedies. The crisis over the awareness of God in the world of today is bound up with a certain number of characteristic aspects of contemporary civilization which do, in fact, give rise to real difficulties. Although these difficulties are not insoluble, we must not minimize them.

One primary question crops up very often and it is this: is there an antagonism between scientific development and religious faith of such proportions that faith retrogresses as man continues more and more to discover scientific explanations for the world? It is a serious question, for it is certain that what characterizes contemporary culture is the very important part that science in its various forms — mathematics, physics, chemistry, and biology — plays in it. It would be absurd to resent in any way this development of scientific thought in its twofold aspect, both speculative, as it explains to us more and more of the world in which we live, and practical, as its technical applications achieve extraordinary results that lessen man's toil and make human life happier.

I would like to point out that what is peculiar to the present moment of scientific development is the development of the human sciences. And this brings us face to face with new and different problems. What basically are the human sciences? They attempt to apply methods that have succeeded very well in the world of nature to a new object, namely, man; they are an attempt to make man an object of science. The attempt is legitimate in itself, for science has the right and the duty to go to whatever limits it can reach, and if there is one thing that scientists of today are very convinced of (and Christians are more and more sharing this conviction), it is that one never has the right to limit the autonomy of scientific research as such. We have had a few examples in the past, with Galileo in particular, which, I believe, have done away with any desire on the part of the Church to involve herself in such matters. I am speaking now of genuine science and not scientism, the arbitrary constructions that one claims to elaborate on the basis of science, for here there is actually no question of science but of pseudo-scientific theories that do not deserve the slightest respect.

Nor am I saying that the rights of science are unrestricted as to its technical applications: this, too, is another question entirely. For it is only too obvious that in the matter of the technical applications of science we meet the human problem. And some of the most basic problems of man's conscience today have to do precisely with this matter of the limitations of the rights of technology in reference to human problems. Two typical examples would be the use of atomic energy for instruments of destruction and the use of anti-conceptual means to restrict births. These two examples are characteristic of points where the development of technology and the question of its use on the plane of the human person interact. It is not my intention here to solve these problems but simply to point out this confrontation between the progress of technology and its application to the domain of man.

Having said that, it is certain that scientific thought will increasingly and daily impregnate the culture in which the man of today is more and more immersed. Now, this fact poses problems from the viewpoint of religious faith, because the man formed by scientific methods is accustomed to attributing certitude to the criteria of these methods. His first temptation will be to claim that science will gradually succeed in explaining what has been called the "religious fact" by purely natural reasons, whose nature we do not know. But to explain the mystical experience of St. Paul or of St.

Teresa by the sublimation of the suppressed eros cannot be taken seriously, for if one thing is clear it is that mystical experience has absolutely nothing to do with the sublimation of an unsatisfied sexuality. I have never seen an atheist seriously maintain that the phenomenon "Jesus" is explained by the contradictions of the economic life in the first-century Palestine and that we can explain him in terms of class struggle, for it is all too obvious that this is ridiculous in view of what the person of Jesus really represents.

But there is another much more subtle attitude which consists not in eliminating the religious fact but in saying that it belongs to the sensory order and that it is therefore purely subjective. The danger here lies in the implication that from now on there can be no such thing as certitude in the religious order because only the sciences can give us true certitudes. As a matter of fact, this is not the case, for there are different levels in reality and there is a type of certitude that corresponds to each of these levels. Pascal has admirably said that there is the mathematical mind to know the things of the body, the intuitive mind to know the things of the heart, and the prophetical mind to know the ultimate realities of man's destiny. We will never attain the certitudes of the heart by means of science; the human person is an abyss that is inaccessible to scientific investigation; it is a mystery that can be known only through being revealed. The philosopher Max Scheler said that secrecy was the distinctive attribute of persons; and it is only in the exchange called love — giving this word its greatest meaning, that is to say, the desire to communicate oneself to another — that we can penetrate this secrecy in the depths of another being. It must be added that the essential certitudes of existence depend in no way on scientific methods: they depend on the confidence that we know we can have in the word of a loved one. And this is the basis of a type of absolutely valid certitude. On a higher plane, when it is no longer a question of knowing the person of others but of opening oneself to what transcends every human person, to that abyss which is the abyss of God, it is all too obvious that there also it would be absurd to think that one could discover certitude by way of a mathematical demonstration or of a cosmic exploration. We can discover God only in so far as God communicates himself in a revelation that has its source in love; and this is a mode of access to supreme truth, absolutely valid when the intellect is used to its fullest.

It must, however, be added that it is very often in minds formed by scientific methods that we see a resurgence of faith today. Paul VI has remarked that faith is reappearing today no longer on the frontiers of science but in the very heart of the scientific man through the discovery he is making of the universe which his science brings to light. Starting with this very world, he discovers a stepping-stone to the ascent toward God. How can a universe that I am discovering through my science that is so permeated with intelligibility not be the product of an intellect? Where there is something intelligible, there is an intellect. And this is indeed what Sartre by a counter-formula confirms when he writes: "The world is absurd; God therefore does not exist." Now, any discussion must begin with the first statement. Is it true that the world is absurd?

If the world is absurd, then I agree with Sartre that God does not exist. But what I absolutely challenge and what the great scientists of today challenge is that the world is absurd, for it looms before us quite to the contrary as extraordinarily penetrated with intelligence. At that moment, if the world is not absurd, Sartre is obliged to admit that God does exist. And it is exactly for that reason that scientific thought is one of the ways whereby the rediscovery of God is in the process of taking place. I have more confidence today in scientific thought rediscovering God than in a literary thought that is very corrupt. There is more health today in scientific thought because scientific thought is directed toward a certain objectivity and does not allow one to say whatever he pleases. This is one point that I would like to stress: if science causes difficulties for faith, it can also bring one back to faith. We are always coming back to the same question: scientific thought hurls a challenge at the religious man, but the question consists in knowing whether the religious man will accept the challenge of scientific thought; something that he can do perfectly. But I object to the statement that the development of scientific thought forces religion to take a step backward. On the contrary, I believe with Teilhard de Chardin that "the more man becomes man the more will he feel the need to adore." This statement definitely pulverizes those who say: "The more man becomes man the less will he feel the need to adore." In this matter, I share the hope of Teilhard: I believe that the man of the twenty-first century will be an even greater adorer because the world he will have discovered will be filled with many more wonders than the one we of the twentieth century have known.

I will add further, by way of conclusion to this matter of the dialogue between religion and science, that there is another point with which the man of science is today confronted. I refer to the problem of men's final destiny. The man of science, in fact, is increasingly and inexorably a responsible man, that is, science is no longer something that one can cultivate in a purely speculative fashion; we cannot stop it from having practical applications, and at that point, the man of science feels responsible for the practical applications of his discoveries. That was Oppenheimer's tragedy. He asked himself whether he had the right to go through with the fission of the atom once he knew it could be used to manufacture instruments of destruction, the like of which mankind had never known. It is impossible, of course, to impede the progress of science, but the very serious problem that the scientist of today is forced to face is this: if he is to further science, he is by that very fact obliged to take great care in the use he makes of it. Now, what does being responsible mean if not being able to refer these applications of science to finalities that regard the human person? Here, then, the scientist is obliged to note that science and technology do not resolve the problems of man, for science and technology are in themselves perfectly equivocal, and can be used for better or for worse. So the question arises as to what, beyond science and technology, may be said of the direction in which science and technology must progress, and here we come face to face with the problem of man.

This brings us to a second type of difficulty confronting the religious man of today, a difficulty no longer stemming from scientific thought but from a willful desire for total freedom. The phenemenon of atheism is the temptation of modern man. The reason for this is the bond which man sets up between the development which is proper to him, namely, his emancipation in regard to a set of servitudes to which he had been bound in the past, and the highest emancipation, his emancipation with regard to God, so that he ends up saying: man becomes fully man only when he is able to do without God, just as the child becomes an adult only when he is able to do without his parents and care for himself. It is precisely this thought that constitutes the basic statement of modern atheism, whether it be the atheism of Marx, existentialist atheism, or almost any form of atheism. Here again we must admit that there are altogether valid data at the basis of this statement. It is perfectly true that man, perhaps for the first time in his history, is experiencing his gradual mastery over the world of nature and, from this point of view, the most unlikely hopes are being held out to him today. The exploration of the planetary world has begun; the mastery of the world of life is one of the fundamental aspects of present-day scientific research.

The man of today feels that he is in the process of freeing himself from thousands of years of not only material servitudes but also of sociological servitudes to which he has been a slave. Our age is one of great human progress, as John XXIII admirably pointed out. Our generation has seen the advancement of the colored people; and it is an age when nations have attained adulthood, nations which but a short while ago were reduced to a state of infantilism by reason of their dependence on other nations. Our era is that in which there is an ever-increasing desire on the part of the working class for participation. The ways and means of working this out pose manifold problems. But we do know that this expresses a human aspiration which, in itself, is altogether legitimate because it is more dignified for a man to share the decisions that affect his destiny than to be purely passive. This is equally true of the advancement of women. Woman's condition in the contemporary world has changed; women share in responsibilities in a more autonomous way than in the past, both in the home and in the building of the city. And this, we note, first came about in Christian countries. There is likewise an advancement of youth, and this is more to the point today. Our young people desire to share more in the decisions that concern them and to participate in forming university policies. This again, to be sure, poses problems. But it is incontestable that it is very beneficial for professors to hold discussions with their students and to become acquainted with their aspirations. It would be absurd to regard 1968 as a black year. In the events of the spring of 1968 worthwhile elements cropped up. The important thing is to give them a meaning and not let them be taken over by just anybody for their own purposes.

The danger does not come from the youth but from the bad teachers who direct the aspirations of the youth ideologies that in the end can only be destructive and alienating. I believe that a Catholic, faced with all that is seething in mankind, always has a feeling of joy as he stands before the creation in which God has placed us. This feeling is certainly not easy to come by but it is nevertheless magnificent in its inventive vitality and in its development. Today we admire the great heights mankind has reached, both in its domination of the cosmos and of society. One of the intuitions of today's youth is that one cannot accept what is absurd in human society; they feel a need to rationalize this society which, after all, could be happy; they are impatient with the stupidity of wars and of conflicts which in the last analysis are based on perfectly irrational motivations, such as the will for power and ideological bias. There is something profoundly positive in their positive desire to organize human society and to free men from the sociological slaveries that still hang heavy over them.

In all this there is what the Council called the "signs of the times," and these signs of the times always have positive aspects that we should accept in their reality. That is why we have to accept fully the human advancement of our times. It is normal that this advancement should give rise to difficulties from the religious point of view. In this context I like the word "challenge," because challenge means something that brings about an interrogation and demands a reaction. But, for all that, it would be absurd to think that the movement toward emancipation, the desire to become adult, necessarily leads to atheism. Why should they? Just a short while ago I used an analogy. It compared a son's attitude toward his father, a worker's toward his employer, a citizen's toward the government, to that of man toward God. The analogy is false. It would lead one to think that just as man today works toward equality in every sphere, by the same token he ought no longer to go along with the notion that there is a transcendence above and beyond himself: he himself should be the ultimate value. This is the assertion of a certain atheistic existentialism: "God and man cannot coexist; if God exists, then I do not exist; if I exist, then God does not exist." This amounts to saying that my personal existence and my autonomy, on the one hand, and the existence of God, on the other, seem to be incompatible.

Our answer to this is that in what we can call the "Christian system" transcendence and participation imply each other. Here we find that divine sense of things, outside of which there is nothing real, and where, on the other hand — we know this only too well — we, too, have our role to play. God did not give us a ready-made world; he gave us a world to make; and consequently, our creativity, our initiative, and our responsibility are immense. We are responsible for the future of the world. This does not mean that we are the only ones responsible and that everything depends entirely on us: it depends on God and it depends on us; it depends on us, and that is why our passivity is contrary to the way in which God willed to make things; but it also depends on God; and that is what atheism rejects when it affirms that henceforth we are old enough to shift for ourselves all alone, and that henceforth man's destiny depends exclusively on himself. This is the very basis of the Marxist position. According to the Marxists the fact of believing in God is a way of depriving the earthly city of energies necessary for its realization; religion is, as it were, an opium. This is also Sartre's position. For him my freedom at every moment is the absolute beginning. Nothing exists before me; my freedom is origin, is creation, is principle; I can do all things and everything depends absolutely on me. What is so serious about the present-day situation is that almost all of our literary culture is permeated with this spirit. Youth is bathing in a culture that is essentially the expression of an atheism of the type we are presently describing. The most disconcerting author for our youth is beyond all doubt Camus, especially because he is such an admirable writer in so many respects, in his reticence and even in his modesty. I am always furious when I read *The Plague*. It too easily justifies the atheist doctor against his interlocutor.

One ultimately rejects all objective moral order as an alienation. The important thing is to be sincere. In the final analysis no importance is attached to the doctrine which a man clings too, but simply to the way in which he carries out his project. Whether a person is a Communist, a liberal, a Catholic, or a Protestant matters not; the important thing is to be a *good* Catholic, a *good* Protestant, a *good* Communist, or a *good* liberal. This attitude is itself contested in certain avant-garde trends, for tolerance does not seem to be the chief virtue of our present-day youth. We are in some danger of finding ourselves tomorrow confronted with something entirely different from syncretism for which all opinions are valid as long as men are sincere. That is not exactly the climate of our college campuses today. But it remains true that what is really important for many young people is that one give one's all, a certain ethic of grandeur, what Malraux admirably expressed in *The Human Condition*. To accept a moral rule is not to be able to shake off the prejudices and conventions of one's milieu. But here we are putting our finger on the tragic error of atheism when it makes rejection of God the condition of man's emancipation.

One extremely evil manifestation of this error made itself felt in May and June of 1969. It confused submission to outside constraints with the recognition of superior values to which one freely subjects oneself. The word "repression" both in reference to the police as well as to morality was all too often used in the year 1968. This identification is scandalous, for it confuses two things which are diametrically opposed. What is most noble in man is the fact that he subjects his freedom to the imperatives of higher values; and, on the contrary, his most degrading quality is to let himself be dominated by the sociological constraints of the milieu in which he finds himself. To this I add that submission to constraint and recognition of higher values are not only dissimilar, they are even contradictory. As a matter of fact, the basis of freedom is the recognition of a transcendence. For as soon as we do away with transcendence, the ultimate court of appeal becomes human authority. Now, there is no greater menace to freedom than a world in which the state, society, the Soviet Union, or the industrial complex determines what is good and what is evil; on the contrary, the guarantee of freedom is that we can always appeal from human judgments to the court of God by which human courts will in the end be judged. What makes me, a Christian, a free man, is that I know that in the end I do not have to give an account to

Nixon, to Mao, or to Brezhnev; that the only one to whom I will have to account is God, who will judge Brezhnev, Mao, and Nixon. The great guarantee of freedom consists in knowing that all the heads of state are only creatures who will be judged by their deeds. The fact that I can appeal to this judgment is what alone guarantees freedom. There is no world more repressive than one in which societies have the last word on the destiny of persons. This existence of a divine tribunal is the only thing that gives objective foundation to the profession of my freedom.

The last point which I wish to stress is that these difficulties with regard to God are met not only outside of Christianity but also within it. This is the most striking fact today. Because, as long as we are dealing with a defiance from without, the situation is normal and even healthy. But it becomes dramatic if we are not able, if the Church is not able, if Christianity is not able to accept the challenge because Christianity is in the process of disintegrating from within. In other words, the most serious problems confronting the Church today are not the problems which she encounters from without but those she confronts from within. We are obliged to take note of a certain crisis of faith within the Church. We know the many difficulties the youth of today in particular are having along these lines; and by way of echo we also know of other countries where the situation is often more serious than in our own. How many are leaving the priesthood, the religious life, and even the Church! That is the gravest problem, and it fills the heart of Paul VI with anguish, and rightly so. We may wonder whether this aftermath of the Council, which could be a magnificent period in this encounter of Christian faith and the modern world, is not, on the contrary, in danger of becoming a period of collapse, a period in which the faith and the life of the Church will disintegrate.

That is why it is important, as of now, to clarify things and to see where these dangers are to be found within. Here I am talking exclusively about the problem that interests me, that is, the problem of God. It is this problem which today is being raised to the extent that we are witnessing a plethora of books dealing with "the death of God," the end of religions, which tell us that we are headed for an epoch of post-religious Christianity. This is what one of the authors of this school, Van Leeuwen, explains when he says that religion is basically a fact of culture that is connected with a pre-scientific state of humanity but now that we have entered into the scientific age, religion will disappear and the problem will be what to do with Christianity when religion will be no more. This may seem strange but it is precisely the problem in question. It is what Francis Jeanson, in his little book, *The Faith of the Unbeliever,* explains quite laconically and graciously to Christians: he tells them that Christianity can still have a future if it does away with God. An atheistic Christianity may still have a future, that is to say, a Christianity that reduces itself to a certain style of relationships between men. This, as I express it in this theoretical way, may seem paradoxical: but all we need do is ask a certain number of people what Christianity consists of. Many would answer: "Christianity consists in loving one's neighbor." The answer is not false, to the extent in which it is true that love of neighbor is constitutive of Christianity, but, on the other hand, it is absolutely false to say that love of neighbor is the totality of Christianity. To do so is to reduce Christianity to a word I do not particularly like, namely "horizontalism," which sees in Christianity only the horizontal dimension of one's relationship to others, completely eliminating one's vertical relationship to God.

We would soon have a Christianity in which the act of going to Mass would not have the slightest importance as long as one participated in union meetings. This is exactly what happened in May, 1968, when leaflets were distributed on the road leading to Chartres and students were told: "What good are you accomplishing by going to Chartres? You'd do far better manning the barricades." At that time I wrote an article in the newspaper *La Croix* in which I said that, if it is a duty to participate in some legitimate social or political action, it is also a duty and an equally important one to go to Chartres, for it is just as important to pray and to manifest one's relationship to God as it is to engage in social or political action. Present-day Christianity is faced with the dangen of becoming secularized, of becoming worldly, of being no more than a variety of socialistic humanism. That is not what the world needs; and if that were the only contribution Christians could make, they would soon be rejected and rightly so, for, after all, from the beginning of the world we have always had socialists, moral professors, and social organizers: they have been helpful, but they never saved anyone.

What the man of today needs is not a little more organization or sociability. What he needs is a Savior. The man of today needs someone who has an answer for the basic problems of his existence which no social organization will ever provide. It would be folly if Christians, belatedly again, were to chase after a Christianity that would be no more than social humanism at a time when the men of our day are beginning to discover its inadequacies and are again beginning to hunger for God. It would be a most distressing spectacle to see men ask for God from a Church that is no longer able to give him God. I know whereof I speak from the point of view of youth. There is in the crisis of May, 1968, a sense of the inadequacy of technocratic society to resolve human problems and a revolt both of the imagination and of the heart which demands that we give an answer to the basic problems — to the problem of happiness, to the problem of the meaning of life, and to the problem of truth. It is essentially this dimension that the men of our time are going to ask of us. It is, therefore, heartbreaking to see Christians and even priests ignore this dimension and thereby reduce Christianity to social action which is altogether laudable but which only represents the degraded aspect of what Christianity is in its wholeness and authenticity.

This partial view of Christianity also expresses itself on the collective level, in what is called secularism, a collective expression for what we have called horizontalism on the individual plane. What, in the final analysis, is secularism? It is the idea that we must reconcile ourselves to the fact that the civilization of tomorrow, as civilization, will make no room whatsoever for God or for the sacred, and that we should resign ourselves to living in a humanity that will be a humanity totally and exclusively profane. To accept this lightly, as a certain number of Christians and theologians do today, is criminal, for, in a society whose whole structure and customary behavior is atheistic, a few mystics could certainly exist, and they could bring about a few conversions; there could still be a few islands of monks. But something will be inexorably and definitively lost: the Christian people. For all men depend inexorably and normally on the milieu in which they live; it is always possible for certain more or less heroic people, for some militants, to assert themselves against their milieu, but it is normally impossible for the mass of men to do so. We can in our day, for example, give a young suburban working girl a

Christian education but it is almost impossible for her, unless she is a heroine, to preserve her faith and her purity in a hostile social world.

So the problem — and this is one of the basic problems of today — is to know whether we accept the idea that the Church of tomorrow will consist solely of small chapels, of small cells, of small militant groups but will no longer be the immense people of the poor. The Christianity of the parish is, of course, that of the militant, but it is also that of the poor man who perhaps does not go to Mass every Sunday, but who insists that his children belong to the Church of Jesus Christ and who would not think of not receiving the priest's blessing before appearing before God. That is the immense mass of the poor which constitutes the authentic Church of Jesus Christ, not a small chapel, or a small number of elite, but that Church which welcomes all men without distinction. This is the Church that I love, this is the Church that I desire for tomorrow and, that she may be possible tomorrow, I must absolutely refuse as a hypothesis (which, however, is not obligatory) that this world of tomorrow be a society that is necessarily secularized and atheistic. Consequently it is our duty to see to it that within this world of tomorrow the religious dimension be also present within the city itself so that the masses of men may again have access to it.

This is tantamount to saying that either on the individual level or on the collective level an attitude of defeatism with regard to the future of God in the souls of men, and in particular in the souls of Christians, constitutes the cankerworm within the Church. What is needed, of course, is a faith full of vitality and dynamism in the presence of certain difficulties which we meet today. That is why we have to struggle even within the Church — and this is not always an easy battle —

to preserve the place we give to God in our personal lives, despite the difficulty that this presents, and on the collective level to take a stand when these basic attitudes seem to us to be unlawfully contested. This is one of the aspects of the way in which the problem of God is formulated concretely in the contemporary Church. The question before us now is this: how can we today, in the world of our time, present the reality of our faith in God in a way that will be convincing for the men of our time?

that there is such a thing as a lie and such a thing as the truth. And even when we lie, we know that we are going against something that nevertheless continues to impose itself on us. Just as in the matter of good and evil, so too we are not the ones who decree what is true and what is false. What is true and what is false compels our recognition and we feel obligated to submit ourselves to it; otherwise, as Pascal says, "not only are we wicked, but we are stupid"; we are someone who refuses to conform his mind to a reality that exists outside of him. When I acknowledge that there is such a thing as objective reality that imposes itself on me, I acknowledge something which my desire for independence, for self-sufficiency, for belonging revolts against — but it is undeniable that this is part of my own experience.

There is also the wound caused in me by the encounter with what is truly beautiful and worthy of love. When I have listened to a wonderful sonata, when I have admired a very beautiful countryside, something in me is, as it were, changed and converted; and I know very well that this deep wound was caused not by that particular thing, the sonata or the countryside, but rather through it I love beauty for itself through a conversion to something that surpasses everything that any finite thing can give me. And this is also the experience of genuine love. When I truly love, something is awakened in me through the person whom I love and goes beyond that person; it is the very discovery of love as such; and that is why all genuine love of itself gives rise to a certain thirst for a reality that transcends it, sets up, as it were, a sort of invitation and awakens in me the nostalgia for an absolute love.

Contemporary man attempts to contest all this, and at all the levels that we have just examined. He may say that all this is in the final analysis the creation of my mind, the invention of my imagination, with no source other than myself. There is today a basic issue of good and evil, involving an enormous effort on man's part to do away with obedience to a law that transcends him. But this issue is truly serious, and do we not very often find beneath this dispute over good, under a certain form, what we have denied under another form? A man, like Sartre, for example, who radically contests the existence of an objective good and evil, who tells me that my freedom is the root of everything, will be the first to rediscover a certain ethic when he sits in judgment over others, when he again sets up a scale of values on the level of the opposition between this or that political ideology. In fact, everyone judges according to different ethics, but still in a certain frame of reference to things that one knows are good and to things that one knows are bad. We may be mistaken as to what is bad or what is good; we cannot deny that there is evil and there is good.

The same holds true for truth. Father Urs von Balthasar, in an excellent little book entitled *Cordula,* recently recalled to mind what the martyrs of bygone days were, and said that today there is the risk of there being no more martyrs because no one any longer believes in the truth. It is true that there are men who died for the truth and who thought that they had to bear witness to it even at the peril of their lives. Were these men taken in by an illusion? Was the ideal to which they commited their life an absurdity? And lastly, are all opinions simply equally valid? Is there nothing worthwhile that we can give ourselves to wholeheartedly and promote with all our being?

The same may be said of love. When I give myself to someone with the certitude that there is an eternal significance in that love, that what I attain transcends my

THE FOUNDATIONS OF OUR BELIEF IN GOD 29

of basic human experience. Next, we shall approach him from the level of the great religions of humanity, and we shall show how all these religions are a true approach to God, although they are always more or less mixed with errors and inadequacies. Then we shall approach God as Scripture reveals him to us, the God of revelation, as he expresses himself in the Old and New Testaments, the Triune God. Next, going one step farther, we shall see how this knowledge of God is continued through the teaching of the Church and theology which is an explicitation of Scripture. And last of all, we shall return to the experience of the mystics, to the testimony that the great witnesses of God give us, and this will bring us back to that more personal contact with the living God. All that we will have said should verify our right to consider this as not simply a question of a subjective experience but as a universally valid truth for all men, of which, consequently, we can be certain.

The important thing — and here I am more especially thinking of what dialogue with unbelievers can be for us — is to begin with what seems to be unquestionable to all men. We sense that the great problem of our day is that all too often discourses about God, even by theologians, skirt the true-to-life experience of men and give an impression of artificiality and abstractness. What is the great problem of catechesis, of preaching, and of theology today? It is speaking to the men of an era, not on the plane of language, which is secondary, but by reaching the heart of man and specifically the heart of the man of today. God speaks to the heart. By "heart" we do not merely mean man's affections, but man in his deepest self. The heart is what Augustine speaks of when he says: "Our heart is restless until it rest in you"; the heart is what Pascal speaks of when he calls to mind the God who is "felt by the heart"; it is what Peguy speaks of when he tells the sinner that he "is far from home, far from the hearth"; the heart is the inner man, the man down deep. The essential problem is to reach the depths of this man, to reach the fundamental experiences of man and more specifically of the man of our time.

Where can we begin? First of all, with what constitutes an experience common to all men, namely, the fact of admitting that we are bound by certain demands, and bound by the heart. Men acknowledge that they do not decide things in a final way, but that they encounter within themselves a certain inner resistance, which is in them more than themselves. Since they experience this something, they cannot dispose of it freely. For example, our experience of the good is in the fact that we observe in ourselves that there are things that we do not have the right to do and others that we have the right and duty to do, and that when we do what we do not have the right to do, we know that we are going counter to something that is holy and sacred, which we cannot help respecting at the very moment we are violating it. It is precisely this that makes us aware that we are sinners. Now, what constitutes this resistance which we meet at the very center of ourselves? It is not something imposed on us from without. It is rather something that we find in ourselves, and yet does not come from ourselves since we experience the fact that we do not dispose of it. I am all too aware that I am not the one who decides what is good and what is evil. I do not feel free to make use of things as I choose and at my discretion and, when I do, I know that I am going against something which in reality continues to assert itself in me in the depths of my being.

There is what we call truth. We know that there are things that are true and things that are false. We know friend of mine, a journalist, André Frossard, published a book entitled *God Exists: I Have Met Him,* in which he recounts his experience. He sprang from an unbelieving family; his father was a politician, a well-known socialist. André remained an atheist until he was twenty. Then one day he entered a church and encountered God. This was for him the most unquestionable evidence of all.

God is just as close to us; that is, perhaps, the very first thing a child knows, and all of us know how wonderful is this knowledge of things divine which we find in children. Even those who do not recognize the face of God in any of his expressions are not always bereft of any experience of him. That is what the writer Emanuel Berl said: "I have not met the face of God which my heart is looking for in any form of religion." Very often one or the other expression of God may embarrass us. But this does not mean that deep down within ourselves we do not know what sort of face we are seeking. Therefore, this experience of God is much more universal than we think; it is implicit in many of our experiences and, very often, we know God without recognizing him. For there are areas in our experience that express him and are related to him without our knowing how to recognize his hidden face in them.

Is this as far as we may go? Many Christians today are tempted to think that the important thing is to bear witness to this experience. Now, this is absolutely insufficient. It is indispenable that we be able to experience God intellectually in order to be able to justify this experience of God before those who contest it. It is too easy to say: "That is my experience" and to stop there. At that moment the unbeliever will retort: "Well, that is not my experience." And then no dialogue will be possible. Christians all too often refuse to enter into this dialogue, not only on the plane of subjective experience but on the plane of objective reality, about which it is perfectly possible to show that it corresponds to a certain number of avenues of research, of convergences, so that belief in God is profoundly reasonable. One of the betrayals of contemporary Christianity is to have abandoned too often these great expanses of the intellect; one of the great evils from which our present-day youth is suffering is that we have left these dimensions too much to thinkers who are almost entirely atheists. We are tragically and all too late discovering what a mistake this has been. There has certainly been a great deal of devotion, of generosity, of good works, and of charity on the part of Christians, but there has also been a great deal of negligence as to the importance of being able to explain the very rational basis of their faith in the present-day situation of the world.

And this is precisely the work that develops upon us: to ask ourselves what our faith in God is based on, what it rests on, and if it is steadfast. We have to put it to the critical test of all that we can array against it, for if the faith of so many Christians today is quite fragile, it is because they have not reflected on it; and it is all too often in this sense at the mercy of critics. Now, the faith we have, the faith that we communicate, must be a faith that, tested in the fire of discussion, has become aware that it bears up perfectly under attack and can fully and in all certitude stand fast before the intellectuals of our time. We can attain such faith — and this is what we shall try to do — from different approaches, for there are many ways by which one can go to God. One person may prefer one way; another person, a different way; the main thing is not to exclude either one.

We shall first speak of approaching God from the level

II: The Foundations of our Belief in God

I have shown how the problem of God is currently at the center of the questions about the future of man and that, in the last analysis, this problem, in its deepest sense, will be the point of confrontation between the two divisions of men — those who think that the disappearance of God is the prerequisite of man's fulfillment and those who think that this fulfillment will come about only in an ever-deeper relationship with God.

We must now approach the very heart of the matter. We never do so without trembling, for it is always difficult to talk about God, and we are very conscious of the fact that what we can say is always so deficient in the face of what he is. Our fear is that what we have to say will blur the problem rather than shed light on it. We perceive the immense distance that lies between our poor human words and the wonder we shall be trying to express. We might be tempted to remain silent, and yet speak of God we must. There is a silence that is good, the silence our soul aspires toward when it prefers to encounter God in solitude and prayer rather than express him in words: such is the silence of contemplation and of the heart-to-heart talk of man with his God. But there is a silence that is evil, the silence of Christians or of men of other religions who no longer dare to speak about God, who have, as it were, a kind of human respect, an unhealthy fear which gives the impression that there is a conspiracy of silence which is extending even to God in our day. This silence must be broken; it is our obligation to be witnesses of God. The objection that we hear and that we ourselves voice, namely, that we must be worthy of speaking about God, has absolutely no justification, for if we waited until we were worthy in order to speak of God, who would ever dare speak of him?

But what is reassuring on this score is the fact that, when we speak about God, we are not preaching about ourselves; the man who speaks about God and who judges in God's name who men are condemns himself at the same time he judges others. In other words, to speak about God is as much speaking to oneself as it is speaking to others; in this sense it rises above all obstacles in order to place ourselves in the presence of what transcends all of us.

What we are tempted to do, and this is entirely understandable, is to bear witness to our own experience. It is true in a sense that this is essential. The important thing is the personal encounter which each one of us has had with God, and the extraordinary, marvelous, undeniable character of this encounter. The most authoritative voices are those of the great witnesses. When Francis of Assisi speaks of God and sings the "Canticle of the Sun," when Teresa of Avila speaks of God and explains the mysterious conversations her soul had with the God who lived in her, there is a sort of incontestable evidence in their tone of voice. A what kind of a man is he who does not lose the zest for life the day he renounces membership in that reign of love and firmly and absolutely encloses himself within his own shell? Here we are at the level of the "heart," that is, at the level of the interior man, and it is at this heart level that the drama of the encounter with God, of the adhesion to God or the refusal of God, is situated.

Let us, therefore, say that the deep-rootedness of this experience into what gives life meaning can also help us to see how God represents the very foundation of reality, which exists in a soverign way. From this point of view, to admit that God exists is to experience reality, and not to acknowledge God is to be living a lie. If God is really the one who sovereignly exists, if God is that fullness of beauty, that fullness of goodness, that plentitude of existence, we begin to realize that the basic and radical sin of the world is to attach so much importance to what has no importance and to attach so little importance to what does have importance. And if to be intelligent is to know things as they are and to give them their rightful place, we must have the courage to say with Scripture that "the fool says in his heart: 'there is no God'" (Ps. 53, 1). For not to acknowledge God amounts to a lack of intelligence insofar as the very nature of the exercise of the intellect is to know reality. Such is the case of the intellect on the physical, human, and metaphysical levels, that is, on the levels of ultimate realities. And from this point of view, let us repeat, one of the prejudices of these times is the belief that it is more intelligent to be an atheist than to be a believer. This is precisely the level at which the problem must be posed: we absolutely refuse to say that belief in God belongs solely to the order of feeling and of consolations and that it does not belong to the order of intellectual and rational confrontation. Quite the contrary, we state that his predication of God arises

from the full exercise of the intellect itself. We do not
have to stop at this level by taking refuge in the domain
of feeling and experience and by abandoning to atheism
the plane of intellectuality and of reason. The young
people are right in their search for deep convictions,
and if they do not find anything that seems convincing
to them when faith in God is presented to them, they
will let themselves be won over very easily by atheistic
ideologies. I am bound to say this to Christians, for
Christians are too often not sufficiently convinced of it;
too often they do not attach enough importance to what
depends on the domain of the intellect, too often they
content themselves with charity and experience; and
there is a certain distrust of the intellect throughout the
Christian world. I believe that this is today the most
tragic of all errors; that is why our duty is the ability
to ratify on the plane of reflection what we believe to be
so fundamental on the plane of experience.

The two, moreover, are never to be separated, and this
predication that God is he who exists in a sovereign way
is also what the real experience of God causes us to discover. St. John of the Cross says that God is darkness
because his light is so resplendent that we cannot stand
its brilliance and that in some way it burns our eyes.
If God is invisible, the reason is not because he is obscurity but rather because his light is too intense. If God
came too close to us, we could hardly bear his presence
so intense, we may say, is his depth of existence; that is
what the biblical text means when it says with admirable
depth: "We cannot see God and not die."

It is at this level that we must again find this intense
reality of God. When we do, we have, as it were, the
feeling that we were surrounded with illusion and lies,
that even the things in our life were no longer in their
rightful place. I mention lies because we are in a world

so afraid to accept God, because of a basic reaction of self-defense. They are afraid of being threatened in the total freedom of ordering their lives, of depending solely on themselves. This is true at all levels. It is true first of all on the level of the intellect. To accept God is to accept the limitations of one's intellect, or what St. Paul called "the obedience of faith"; it is to admit that the norm of my intellect is not my own reason, but the truth of God, and that, consequently, I must not conform things to my intellect but conform my intellect to things, that is to say, subject myself to reality. My thoughts turn to that text of Claudel that so profoundly expresses the sense of adhesion to reality, of submission to reality: "You have put the horror of death in my heart; my soul does not tolerate death; I am living in your abominable night, I lift my hands in the trance and transport of savage and deaf hope; he who no longer believes in God no longer believes in beings and he who hates creatures hates his own substance."

There is, therefore, a transformation whereby refusal takes precedence over consent, whereby the fundamental attitude no longer is yes but no, whereby what takes precedence is essentially the desire to assure the autonomy of my freedom. Now, I can take upon myself the autonomy of my freedom only by rejecting God, for to accept God is to accept a limitation, not merely the limitation of another creature who enters into my life, but an absolute limitation to the sovereignty of my freedom. This limitation is not something that destroys it, for my freedom cooperates with the freedom of God, but something which nevertheless brings it about that I am no longer completely master of myself. This is true, and it is even more true when we pass into the realm of action. The reason why men too often stray from God is that they refuse to accept his law, refuse to subject their lives to the will of God.

The whole history of our spiritual life begins from the moment when we say to God: "My will be done," until the moment when we finally understand that we should be saying just the opposite. True good consists in doing God's will and not in God's doing ours. But this is precisely where the profound and radical reason for the rejection of God is situated not in non-experience of God — such experience is almost universal — but on the level of the heart that refuses to recognize a transcendence implying inevitably a dependence at all levels. And yet it is this relationship to God that alone gives consistency and value to my life. What, after all, does it teach me? That God attaches importance to my life; that, however lonely my life may be, there is someone for whom I do exist, that what I do is not indifferent; that the least act of fidelity causes God to look at me with love and that every infidelity wounds God in the love he has for me. My life takes on value and assumes a dramatic meaning, since at every moment it involves this drama of love between God and me. It can be said that life took on meaning with Christianity because the value of every life has importance for God.

There is, therefore, a whole order of relationships between the living God and the living person. This set of relationships disturbs me in my possessive will and threatens me in my desire for belonging and in that thirst for complete self-determination which is so profoundly imbedded in the heart of modern man. But at the same time I also perceive in a mysterious way that ultimately this is the most wonderful of all realities because it is the absolute of love that snatches me from myself, a rescuing that, deep inside, I desire above all else. What kind of a man is he who, deep within himself, does not aspire to a certain absolute love? And desire to help him fulfill himself in accordance with what is best in him; and in my love of the other I refer again to an order that transcends him. I cannot escape this demand without betraying myself, without in the end repudiating all that I believe in. There is, therefore, a plane where this value that thrusts itself on me and the personal character of all that transcends me come together and where what constitutes these values can only be a personal reality that transcends what human persons are, namely, a personal and living God in whom I recognize this beauty, this goodness, this truth which I sought through creatures as fulfilled in a person. These values must finally be fulfilled in him so that everything else will make sense; and if he does not exist, nothing has any more meaning, for everything I believed in, everything for which I gave my life when I served a cause, when I truly loved, when I believed in beauty, would ultimately be only an immense illusion that would finally vanish before the absurdity of death. All the values I believe in have no meaning, no reason or solidity if they do not have a basis and a justification in an objective and transcendent reality.

Here, then, we have a fundamental question on the meaning of life, and the simple answer to that question is God; everything on which I believe I have the right to base my life and to pledge my life is essentially justified through him. As soon as God does not loom on the horizon, everything is all one. In an absurd world, absolutely nothing has any importance; in a world where there is no term to which values can be referred, they are no more than the expression of one behavior among others, since ultimately there is not one justification that will be given them. We can therefore say that God here is conceived of as being the basic ground of all that is essential in my intermost experience. St. Augustine said that God is more in me than I am, that is to say, when I enter into myself and seek the basis of my existence in all its fundamental choices, I become aware that beyond myself I meet that on which I can lean, from which I derive support, that on which I can base myself so that everything makes sense. For many contemporary Christians, it is this very ground that is shaky. They have the impression of being on sand; they carry within themselves certain aspirations, but they do not have the feeling that they are based on anything solid; that is why they have so little confidence in their personal certitudes and in the witness they must bear toward others. As long as we have not given our faith this solid foundation in God and as long as it does not go beyond the level of certain experiences, certain habits, certain tendencies, it remains very superficial. We certainly sense that we could not do without it, but, at the same time, that we are absolutely incapable of making serious use of a dialogue with an atheist. There is absolutely no question here of a kind of demonstration from without, but rather of encountering what is innermost in the heart of man and of showing that what is innermost in the heart of man has no justification and reality without reference to a living God.

The objection may be advanced: why are not all men convinced of this? The answer is because love is frightfully involving, because love is always upsetting, and it is always dangerous to bring someone else into one's life. This is true of human love. From the moment we begin to love we know that we will never belong to ourselves, and it is a terrible and at the same time a delightful bond, the expression of a profound appeal, and at the same time — as we know — a very great slavery. It is even more dangerous when this someone is God, for we never know what this can lead to. That is why men are fragile and passing existence, that it is something other than a mirage of life, am I at that moment a victim of illusion? Does all that in the long run make no sense? Or — and this is the basic question — am I right when I believe that this is the underlying meaning of reality? Is the world a momentary illusion that vanishes into nothingness or are there fundamental values whose reality I have experienced within myself and to which I thought that everything else deserved to be ordered if it is to have a solid basis?

At this point the question arises about the meaning of all we have just said. So far we have said absolutely nothing that cannot be discussed on the plane of ordinary experience, at the level of which every man and woman has something to say. It is not a question of anything that is imposed on us from without, but simply of something which I call the witness of the heart. And so calling it, I have to ask myself what this fundamental witness means and implies. In the final analysis, what can justify this witness, give it a foundation; what brings it about that these values which I believed in are not simply a fabrication of my mind but have a reality and a consistency in themselves, that a goodness and truth exist outside of me?

What can exist outside of me and foist itself on me? I recognize only one limitation to my freedom, and that limitation is love, that limitation is the freedom of the other person. There is no more profound experience for me than the fact that I never have the right to make someone else the tool of my pleasures, the slave of my whims, that it is my duty to treat this other person as another self, to wish the freedom of the other person with the same desire with which I want my own freedom, and to desire his fulfillment just as I have the duty to desire my own. We can say that the sacrifice intrinsic to love seems to be something absolutely legitimate and absolutely reasonable, and in no way an alienation. My freedom is not the source, the origin, or the end of everything. There is a limitation that every man certainly admits and accepts, namely, the one which imposes on him the duty of helping others to accomplish what he wants to achieve for himself. It is a basic step, for it shows me that nothing can impose itself on me, that nothing can limit my freedom that in the end is not a personal reality. This personal reality impresses itself on me as deserving of being willed with a will equal to that which I have with regard to myself and my fulfillment.

Now, I am going to bring the two propositions together. On the one hand, I have noted that there is an absolute value that transcends all that I encounter in my ordinary experience, that through everything that is limited and finite, I attain and always pursue something that transcends it. On the other hand, I noted that nothing from without can foist itself on me that is not a personal reality, that is to say, that is not of the same order that I am myself, not a law or an external constraint — I would experience that I always have the right to revolt against such a thing — but a value that urges me from within, which I cannot refuse to adhere to and which I am obliged to will for itself. But this reality cannot simply be the person of others, since by definition it transcends what another can give me and because my love for the other person always leaves me with the same unsolved problem. I desire his well-being, but what is his well-being? His good is something that can be defined only in relationship to something other than his arbitrary freedom. Satisfying the whims of another has never constituted real love. When I truly love someone, I do not desire to give in to all his caprices. On the contrary, I that is a dramatic world, the world of the forces of good and evil, in which we have been victims of some evil spell that diverted us from true goods, from reality, and drove us into the world of illusion. Likewise we must rediscover the true hierarchy of values, put God again into our lives in his rightful place and creatures in their proper place. We must correct in ourselves and in the entire world a sort of radical deformation, the consequence of which is that things are properly speaking upside down and that humanity has become organized around a dream universe by turning itself away from what is genuinely real. Essentially sin consists in not putting God in his rightful place and replacing him with idols, namely, our pleasures, our ambitions, and our curiosities. We understand how speaking to God is essentially facing up to the fundamental options of our lives, not facing up to something that comes and superimposes itself from without but to a reality that dominates them in their most radical depths. And this, once again, we have to try to achieve very poorly, very weakly, very humbly, to the extent of our possibilities and our strength with the idea that this is the way we can gradually, as it were, rectify this warped axis of the human condition. It is at this level that the true revolution is finally situated. This is what Christ tells us when he presents himself to us as "the Way, the Truth, and the Life" (Jn. 14,6), that is, as the one who reveals to us the true meaning of life.

III: Natural Religion
Christian Revelation

We have already dealt with the matter of encountering God on the level of what constitutes the basic human experience. We ask ourselves in what way man was led through his own experience to encounter transcendence and as a result to turn toward God. And we said that this was essentially bound up with the basic experiences of beauty, truth, love, and goodness. In all these experiences, which are common to all normal men, we encounter something in man that transcends man. In other words, we find absolutely no justification for this in ourselves; we know that we are not its source. Yet it makes us sense in ourselves something, or better still, someone who, although quite beyond us, is still alive within us. This we call in a general way the knowledge of God through reason, the natural knowledge of God, for that is what it is. We may give it a more formal, a more logical, a more systematic aspect but, when all is said, the essential thing is that it corresponds to a basic human experience, common to all men. Of course, man is free and he can close his eyes to this experience; it is not our place to judge whether this blocking is due to difficulties that certain people fail to resolve or whether it is the expression of a desire for self-sufficiency which then becomes a denial of God and, consequently, a sin.

But what is basic for us is that this encounter with God forms part of our human experience as such, to which no man is absolutely a stranger and that, from this viewpoint, prior to any revelation or to any encounter with any religion whatsoever, there is a dimension of man which is receptive to the mystery. In other words, as far as we are concerned, a man is truly a man only if he fulfills himself on a threefold level. First, on the level of mastery of the world (this is the wonderful domain of science, both speculative and practical in the area of research); secondly, on the level of communion with others, in all the forms of love, friendship, and all that arises from the spiritual community, with all that pertains to our relationships with others on the institutional level: the social duty, national duty, and the duty of promoting peace. But one who fulfills himself only on these two levels, i.e. the level of scientific knowledge and mastery of the world, and on the level of communion with others, would not be a complete man; he would be lacking something basic. Consequently if any doctrine of man mutilates him in that essential part of his being, we challenge its right to call itself humanism, in the genuine sense of the word. And that is why we believe that a civilization worthy of the name is one that must necessarily make room for the religious dimension of man, if it is true that civilization has no other purpose than to enable humans to fulfill themselves in the totality of their dimensions.

I will therefore say that one of the most fundamental errors in the world of our day and of many Christians of our time is to consider that a civilization can fulfill itself at a purely secular level and even that we must accept that the civilization of tomorrow, as civilization, be a civilization without God; we are even told that the external signs of the sacred ought to disappear: the churches in our cities and religious festivals in the rhythm of the seasons; it is further added that religion ought to become something purely internal, purely individual, exclusively private. This we totally reject in the name of the entire history of humanism which has always seen in the religious genius of all civilizations one of the essential values of what constitutes human civilization. That is why we absolutely repudiate a separatism — which would be the temptation of many men and of many Christians of today — between a secular life that would totally ignore God and a religious life that would be totally severed from secular existence. Instead, the task of today's Christians is first of all to rebuild unity among themselves, the unity of their life as men and the unity of their life as Christians so that, having restored this unity in themselves, they may labor to restore it in the society in which we have to live.

We now take a second step as we tackle the problem of religion and revelation. We have just spoken of the religious dimension of man in itself. We now take up in a more positive way the expressions of this encounter of man with God, and this will bring us to two questions which are crucial for many people. First, we shall treat of the relationships between Christianity and the other religions. Is Christianity truly something different from all the other great religions of the world — Hinduism, Islam, and the major religions of ancient Greece? Is Christianity simply the religion of the western world, and do not Hinduism and Islam offer us equally valid forms of religion? In this context, is it not some kind of unbearable intolerance for Christians to wish, as people claim, to impose their religion on others? Is there something in the missionary apostolate that springs from a kind of lack of appreciation for the value of other religions?

This attitude, which may be termed in a general way as syncretism, is certainly facilitated today by the fact that we are brought in touch with the non-Christian religions, either on the level of human relationship — where we meet Moslems, Jews, Buddhists and are struck by their great religious depth — or on the plane of our reading. By the very fact of this encounter of cultures, a remarkable and wonderful happening in the contemporary world, we are prompted to read the works of this and that Moslem mystic or Indian philosopher; and in them we will surely encounter religious values of undeniable authenticity. Then a question arises in our minds: "After all, are not these men as good as we are? Is it not mere sectarianism on our part to regard our religion as superior to theirs?" We must, therefore, examine the values of the religions — an often unappreciated task — and also locate in relation to this world of religions what constitutes the specificity of Christian revelation.

The first attitude we meet proceeds from a sort of overevaluation of the pagan religions that would lead to equating them with the Christian revelation. But what is odd today is that we also encounter another attitude that derives from the opposite tendency, i.e. to depreciate the pagan religions because they are the expression of a mentality that unduly sacralizes the realities of nature. And we welcome as a blessing the progress of science which destroys this religious mentality, considered as corresponding to an outmoded period of the history of the human mind; this accounts for all the present-day proneness to speak of the end of religion, of the death of God, and of desacralization. All these violent criticisms directed at the sacred, this sympathy for all that is laicized and secularized in the modern world is extended to the very substance of Christianity itself; and it is thought that Christianity must be purified of the religion that subsists in it, in such a way as to reduce it to its pure essence. What is meant by purifying Christianity of the religion that subsists in it? It means to regard the desire to sacralize the essential moments of life, such as baptism, marriage, and death, as so much paganism; it means that when men want to punctuate the year with feasts that correspond to a seasonal rhythm, when they wish to attach special importance to certain geographical places where pilgrimages are made, this is all so much paganism. It would, therefore, attempt in some way to empty Christianity of all that seems to be the survival of a pagan world. We may then ask ourselves what the Christian message will become once religion has disappeared and what a religious Christianity can be. We would be confronted with a Christianity that would be emptied of its religious dimension. Would it not then be in danger of being no more than a sort of morality or social humanism among other social humanism?

It is a paradox that today, at one and the same time, we encounter these two opposing tendencies, and that is why our task is so important, for we must define the status of the religious domain as such. Now, for us this status corresponds to the natural man. Basically, everyone of us is pagan by nature. A newly born baby is neither a little atheist nor a little Christian; he is essentially a good little pagan. By that I mean that because he is a little child of man, he is a tiny creature of God and that for this very reason there is a basic bond between God and him. The child will ratify this bond once his awareness awakens, and he will understand that when people speak to him about God this is a communication to him of a most profound experience. This little child is not a little Christian; he will become one through baptism. As Tertullian, one of the first Christian writers, said: "One is not born a Christian; he becomes one." What was this child before? He was not a little atheist, for atheism is not natural, and a little child is a natural being, and one is by nature pagan. He is, therefore, a little pagan, that is to say, he is situated on the level of a natural relationship with God.

Paganism has a very positive signification. I am thinking particularly of all the content and depth that lies in ancient paganism or in the paganisms of the Orient of today. Furthermore, paganism and atheism must not be confused. A pagan is the very opposite of an atheist. A pagan is someone who injects religion into everything; we may even say that he puts almost too much religion into everything. The pagan is the man who sees divinities everywhere, water-nymphs in fountains or dryads in oak trees. His is an enchanting vision that peoples all of nature, so often made lonely and desolate by science, with a vision of mysterious presences which makes it a sort of enchanted universe. Christianity carries us beyond that; it lifts man above himself and inserts him into a mystery that transcends him. Atheism is below nature; it deprives human nature of that religious dimension, of that relationship to the sacred which is profoundly natural.

To determine this condition of the world of the religious, of the sacred, of the pagan, we shall avail ourselves of the insights of science and in particular of all the important modern works on the phenomenology of religions. Here I am thinking of remarkable, classical works, such as the book *Le Sacre,* by the German, Rudolph Otto, which, in these times of desacralization, seems to be very wholesome, for it is filled with the sense of the sacred. The Rumanian author, Mircea Eliade, treats the same subject in his *Traite D'histoire des Religions*. This book constitutes an admirable phenomenology of religious facts and shows to what an extent encountering God through nature is an element common to all religions of all times and of all places. And lastly, I am thinking of Father Louis Bouyer's book, *Rite and Man*. This, too, gives to the pagan dimension, to that spontaneously religious nature of man, its whole dimension. Naturally, I shall draw on Sacred Scripture, for Scripture is not silent about that moment of human history which is not yet Christian revelation, which is not even yet the revelation of Abraham, but which is what we may call cosmic revelation or the first stage of the history of revelations. For we can say that the history of humanity is the history of successive revelations, each of which constitutes a new advance in the knowledge of God and through which man is lifted up from glory to glory.

The first of these revelations is the revelation of God through the universe. It is the reliability of God as it expresses itself through the regularity of the laws of nature which is the very foundation of cosmic revelation. The problem of paganism in the industrial civilization is a very different problem, and we shall speak of this shortly. But what is basic here is the impression that there is something divine in the regularity of the laws of nature according to which God communicates to man the gifts necessary for his existence. And what the Old Testament affirms, the New Testament echoes. St. Paul, speaking to the pagans of Lystra, proclaiming the good news of Jesus Christ for the first time to these pagans, said to them: "God allowed each nation to go its own way; but even then he did not leave you without evidence of himself in the good things he does for you: he sends you rain from heaven, he makes your crops grow when they should, he gives you food and makes you happy" (Acts 14, 16-18). In other words, even before the gospel fully revealed to us the face of Jesus Christ, God had from the very dawn of man's creation never ceased to reveal himself to all men without exception by giving them rain and fertile seasons and by providing them with food and making them happy. Men of all times have always celebrated the rhythm of the rains and the bountiful seasons as religious feasts, and they always considered eating as a sacred thing in which the bread they ate seemed to them to be a gift and a sign from God.

What, precisely, is the point of all this? Essentially the manifestation of God through creation itself. With Abraham something different appears, namely the revelation of God in history. At that moment, God chose a people, and the destiny of that people took on a special meaning. But before that, revelation, the means by which God revealed himself was essentially creation. There are two books, the book of the world and the book of Scripture. For the pagan, there is still only the book of the world; the world speaks to him of God. And the pagan is the man who senses, who discerns through nature itself, through the world that surrounds him, some sort of mysterious presence that reveals itself to him through a whole universe of signs, symbols, and relationships, that is to say, of manifestations of the sacred. For the whole world speaks of God; the whole world is a hierophany. For example, to men of all religions, to the Egyptians with their god Ra, to the ancient religion of the Chinese and the Greeks, the light of the sun and the heat emanating from it seemed not to be a divinity but rather a kind of sign, a symbol, an expression of the mysterious power which gives light to man and keeps him warm. In the myths of many religions the springs, the moonlight, and the serpent were associated with the mystery of fertility, the mystery of life. In all religions rocks were an eminent hierophany, that is to say, they gave the sense of the divine because they were majestic, because they were immovable and hard, because they were resistant, because they were something one did not dispose of.

I believe that the scientific knowledge of the phenomena of nature is a very valid and admirable strong point. It is our endless duty to make headway in this knowledge of nature. But if the objects of nature have a dimension that originates in scientific knowledge, they also have an aspect that is the result of poetic knowledge; and the same object, approached from these two points of view which are not in any way mutually exclusive, can be fully studied. To my way of thinking the truly intelligent man is one who is able to exercise his intellect at different levels, to approach an object, from its various dimensions, and not one who has locked it in a single dimension by depriving it of a whole area of knowledge it could have brought. That is why I absolutely challenge the statement that the scientific knowledge we get from the universe, simply because it is scientific, necessarily desacralizes the universe. Even if I go to the moon, the crescent of the moon, illuminating the night, will still remain for me the evocative sign of a certain mystery of purity, light, and life. Borman photographed the moon and took away some of our poetic illusions regarding it. But this fact did not prevent him, as he sped away from it, from joyfully rediscovering that beautiful, distant moon that charmed his imagination. This was in no way destroyed by the experimental and somewhat depressing knowledge that he gained about its being composed of a certain number of chemical elements and that in the near future it might be used as a source of coal, gold, or diamonds.

This discovery of God through nature is fundamental, for it is from oppositions such as these that we are told that religion, considered as the pagan attitude of knowledge of God through the universe insofar as science knows the universe, ceases to have a meaning. Now I radically contest this attitude. The truth of poets is just as objective a truth as that of the scientists; they constitute two dimensions of man. One of the great contemporary problems is precisely the danger of a culture that runs the risk of being only scientific and that consequently would deprive our knowledge of the world of an essential dimension and in particular would prevent the world from continuing to be what it has always been for us, that marvelous book that speaks to us of God.

I have spoken of discovering God through nature; I shall now speak of discovering God through the gestures of man. What is a pagan? He is a man who sees something sacred in the essential gestures of human existence. Péguy has written some admirable pages on these gestures of the craftsman which had almost the rhythm of a liturgy, the time when there was something sacred about work, when it had a certain ritualistic aspect about it. It must indeed be said that in an industrial civilization money and automation tend to make the normal course of family life lose its meaning. In all the religions of the world taking one's meal was considered, not as simply the quasi-animalistic satisfying of a need for food, but as the time of family reunion and, at the same time, a kind of thanksgiving to God from whom these blessings had been received. It is certain that the quick meals eaten today in a snack bar are terribly desacralized and I would say are hardly sacralizable, but I do not for one

NATURAL RELIGION — CHRISTIAN REVELATION 53

minute say that this constitutes progress. There are also — and here we put our finger on the most profound and the most human basis of eternal paganism — those essential moments of human life, namely, birth, the entrance into adolescense, engagement, marriage, and then, at the end of a faithful life, the last rites that surround the moment of death.

How can we define the religious man? He is the man who cannot bear, and this from a kind of basic instinct, having the presence of God absent from these essential moments of life. Here we have something sacred that is basically human. It is in this that many Christians of our day are perhaps only pagans. True, Christianity is sometimes lived as the paganism of the western world, but this in itself is something and even a great deal. That is why I defend with all my strength those poor Christian people whose Christianity does not go beyond being faithful to these basic moments, and yet from a secret instinct of a profoundly upright heart, they would find it unbearable, even if they were sinners, if their children were not married in church or were buried without the blessing of a priest. I am not saying that we should not make every effort to see to it that these Christian-pagans become pagan-Christians, that we should not make every effort to see to it that this Christianity which is barely emerging from paganism does not soar toward an authentic Christianity, but I do say that it is Christian-like and humanly basic for me not to be able to accept the absence of the sacred in these essential moments of existence.

This is where we sense the danger of the terrain on which we stand, for it is all too obvious that it is on points like these that many Christians today are at odds. Pure Christianity, the Christianity of militants, of the elite, makes many very legitimate demands on its adherents. But a certain conception of pure Christianity is inclined to disregard the tremendous value of the fidelity of the great majority of the men and women of every country to that basic link with God in the essential moments of life. I must say that these ideas crystalized in me after returning from a trip to Latin America where, contrary to what many say, I was upset by the life of this immense, Catholic continent. When people say to me: "But this Catholicism is a sociological Catholicism," I absolutely contest it, because, despite supersitions and deformations, it corresponds to a basic religious need. I contest anyone's right to hold this religion of the poor and of the humble in contempt. I consider such an attitude as one of the deepest injustices of certain contemporary élite Catholics, among who there can be a great deal of spiritual pride. We certainly need militants, but militants no longer make sense when they attract no great following among the people. And I must say that a church made up of generals does not interest me.

After having spoken of paganism in itself, let us turn our thoughts for a moment to that universe of great religions which are the historical realization of eternal paganism. What greater thing is there in the history of mankind? Human history is certainly the history of the great inventions of science, it is the history of the masterpieces of litertaure; but in the history of India, of China, of Islam, of Israel, of Greece, of Rome, and of Africa, there is nothing more essential than these very religious creations. These creations are normally and eminently different, owing essentially to the difference of the religious genius of the peoples. Here, I am prescinding from the religions "of the Book" (that is, essentially Judaism, Christianity, and Islam which represent a special case); I shall be contrasting them shortly with these worlds of paganism. But what I am speaking of is the ensemble of these great pagan religions. All peoples without exception first began by being pagans and this forms part of the patrimony of each race. An Indian has the Hindu religious genius, an Arab has the Semitic religious genius; an African has the animistic religious genius. All of this constitutes ever so many wonderful and indestructible diversities. Simone Weil, who loved the great religions, was pained at the idea that when Christian missionaries introduced Christianity into a country they destroyed those creations of human genius which the great pagan religions were. She was to a great extent correct, for there is something unacceptable about destroying the religion of a country one wishes to christianize.

For example, it would be treason for an Indian to be obliged to convert himself to a western Christianity. He would then abandon something to which he is legitimately attached, namely, the religious genius of his race. But if, as we shall show, the word of God is independent of all cultures and of all religious geniuses, and if it is received by all peoples and by each race in their own way, we can see that, far from destroying the religious genius of peoples, it leads religious genius to its highest fulfillment. Christianity did not destroy the religious genius of Greece or of Rome. On the contrary, after Christianity had been accepted by these pagans of Greece and Rome, their religious genius was, as it were, purified in that wonderful creation which western Christianity is. Indians, in the same way, must be Christians in the Indian way; Africans must be Christians in the African way; Arabs must be Christians in the Arab way. There is positively no reason why an Indian who becomes a Christian must become a Christian in the English way or why an African has to become a Christian in the French way. That is why all the values of the religious genius of peoples subsist within Christianity. Conversion to Christianity has never meant the betrayal of the religious traditions of one's race, but rather bringing them to a crowning fulfillment.

One more remark before taking up the problem of revelation properly so-called. I have said that all these great religions are expressions of the religious genius of man, that they represent an imperishable aspect of the religious patrimony of mankind, one of its greatest riches. But these religions are also the creations of man. By that I mean they are not religions that have been directly revealed by God. At their very beginning we meet such great religious geniuses as Buddha, Zoroaster, and Confucius. As a result there is always in these religions something syncretistic, and it is here that our initial adversaries have their little word to say. They say to us: "But does not religion consist in sacralizing power and nature; is it not in this sense something that tempers with the reality of things?" True, there is always idolatry in all pagan religions. But just what is idolatry?

Idolatry consists in treating what is merely a creature as divine. We should not think that only the pagans of former times were idolaters. Idolatry is a very widespread phenomenon of our own time and exists under new forms. There is idolatry as soon as we make a human reality, whatever it is, an absolute. But it is true that there was a deformation in these pagan religions when, instead of simply seeing it in the sun or the rain symbols and manifestations of the sacred, they treated these realities as gods. Likewise, rites have a certain value, for example, those rites connected with meals or the seasons of rural civilization, but they also run the risk of becoming a sort of magic whereby one tries to exert pressure on a god; and the magic then seems to be a perversion of what the authentic cosmic liturgy is. On the level of mysticism, that is to say, on the level of what constitutes the inner search for communion with the absolute, there are all the deformations of a certain pantheism which is concerned merely with losing oneself and of being dissolved in an impersonal absolute, a phenomenon we often find in religions such as those of India, religions which do not culminate in an authentic encounter with the living God. We must, therefore, say that not only do cosmic religions, pagan religions, merely represent a first stage in the encounter with God, but that there are moreover always a certain number of deformations or deviations in them.

In view of this, what does the specificity of the biblical and Christian revelation represent? This is the basic question we must ask ourselves. How can we situate it in the universe of religions? One thing is certain: biblical and Christian revelation is not simply one religion among others. We most firmly protest against the idea that would make Christianity the religion of the West, as Hinduism would be the religion of India, Islam the religion of the Arab world and the African religions those of the African world. This is a complete deformation of reality. These pagan religions are always the religions of a race, for they are the expression of the religious genius of a people; and that is why it is absurd to change one's religion. But revelation is in no way the expression of the religious genius of a people: it is essentially something that comes not from man, but from God, and it is perfectly normal to go from religion to revelation. They are two absolutely different matters, because in this case we change from one order to another. It is absurd to go from Indian paganism to African paganism, because they belong to the same order and because it is better to adhere to what corresponds to the tradition of one's own race.

But Christianity is something totally free with respect to all cultures of all races. It is a Word that is proclaimed to all men, of all religions, as a divine intervention having an absolutely universal character that affects the totality of men. It is of the utmost importance that we accurately circumscribe it, for, unless we do so, the meaning of the mission of the Church completely disappears; she would loom as the ambition of the imperialism of an occidental religion that would like to thrust itself on other cultures, and that would be absolutely intolerable. But that is not what the Church is trying to do at all; and if, because of our very vocation as Christians, it is our duty to proclaim the message of Jesus Christ to all men of all religions, that is in no way whatsoever to make us publicity agents for the religion of the West, but rather bearers of the word of God which can be received by all races and by all cultures.

I shall summarize the basic difference between pagan religions and revelation quite briefly: pagan religions are essentially the expression of a movement that rises from man to God. These religions are the expression of that search for God which is written in the heart of man; through religions man tries in an obscure and groping way to discern beyond visible things the invisible and mysterious realities whose existence he has some vague idea of. Revelation is the opposite movement; it does not go from man to God; it goes from God to man. The essence of revelation is that God came to man: it is a gesture of God. Between man and God there is an abyss that man cannot cross. That is why all pagan religions eventually end in a sort of abyss, where they sense their limitations. Nor is it possible to penetrate into this abyss if the abyss itself does not move

NATURAL RELIGION — CHRISTIAN REVELATION

toward us. Now, it is the faith of the Bible that God comes to us. It is an answer to that enormous question formed by the ensemble of religions. Consequently, what characterizes Christian revelation is that first of all it deals essentially with events. For the pagan religions events have no importance: relationship to God is something that is outside time. For revelation the event is basic. If the Word of God has not taken flesh in the womb of Mary, if the Word of God has not raised up from the dead on Easter Sunday, there is nothing else left. Religions exist. People did not await Jesus Christ in order to be religious. It is absolutely unnecessary to be a Christian in order to believe in God. Millions of men believed in God before Christ came on the scene. Christ did not come to teach us that God exists, but rather to reveal to us that God is love; in other words, he came to us, he came in search of us. Consequently there are divine interventions in the course of human history; God is at work in this history; it is he who liberated his people from Egypt, who took flesh in the womb of Mary and who raised this flesh to life; it is he also who is present in the Eucharist and who will come at the end of time to judge the living and the dead. There are certain other events, a certain number of divine interventions in addition to all that and, in that sense, the purpose of revelation is altogether something quite different from the body of beliefs which constitute the substance of pagan religions.

That is why Christianity poses problems different from those of religions. Many men do not have much difficulty admitting that there is a certain mystery into which we plunge, but it is much more difficult to admit the virginal conception, the resurrection of Christ, or transubstantiation. And lastly, a goodly number of errors derive from the fact that many Christians reduce Christianity to religion. After all does it not suffice to believe that God is Mystery and to adore him in silence? But at that moment, we are a religious man, but we are not a Christian. We are Christian the moment we believe that God came on earth, that he assumed our humanity, and that, laying hold of that poor human flesh, unable of itself to cross the abyss that separates it from Transcendence, he transported it, after having laid hold of it, in order to usher it into the depths of God. With that we are in another domain.

The result — and this is another consequence — is that in religions what counts is a sense of religion. In revelation what counts is faith. Christians often confuse the two. We either have the religious sense or we don't. There are people who find mysterious delights in prayer; there are those whom this deeply disturbs. It matters very little. For faith there is but one question: "Is what the gospels say true?" If it is true, it is not a question of sentiment: it is a matter of surrendering oneself to the truth, and we surrender ourselves to the truth without any kind of sentiment. I know people who are totally devoid of all religious sentiment and who are admirable believers, men especially. Conversely, I know people who have religious sentiments to spare and who put them to the worst possible use, for they apply them to the most contestable mystics or to the most mystical arguments, which constitutes a perverted religious feeling, because it has not found its true object. That is why faith is something that essentially derives from the intellect and the heart of men who honestly, lucidly, and humbly surrender themselves to a truth that thrusts itself on them, even if that truth seems to be strange, mysterious, and difficult. This truth imposes itself on the intellect and the heart because Jesus Christ is pictured in the gospel as being a witness absolutely worthy of faith. The important thing is not first of all to experience things but essentially to believe in the word of him who is its witness. And there is only one problem for faith and that consists in knowing whether Jesus Christ appears to us as a witness of a human and divine authenticity such as we have the right (lucidly and exactly as we are required, and not in an attack of despair or in a mode of exaltation) to base our life and thought on. Therein lies the difference between the domain of religious experience, of that obscure search for God by the pagan, and the domain of faith, which consists in confessing that God has come to us, however unlikely that may seem, because the witnesses and signs that point him out to us are undeniable.

One final question remains: what happens to religion in revelation? I have shown that religions correspond to the stage of the natural man, that every man was by nature a pagan; but now revelation ushers us into another universe; will this universe destroy the religious man, abolish the pagan man? Certain Christians today believe it will. A very outstanding, contemporary theologian, Karl Barth, condemns religion. In his writings which draw their inspiration from the doctrine of the Reformation with which he is affiliated, he regards religions as a sort of promethean attempt by man to lay hold of God and radically set him over against faith. In a less profound way many Christians see impure realities in all the natural expressions of religion, in its spontaneous needs to sacralize the essential moments of life, in the sacred character given to the universe from which science is in the process of beneficiently liberating us. They claim that Christianity should be purified of such tendencies and practices. To them the cult we render to the Blessed Virgin and the recitation of the rosary are paganism. We are told that what still subsists in Christian usages — holy water, the crucifix in our homes, candles — is superstition and that we must do away with these impure residues in order to attain a truly pure Christianity, so pure indeed, that it will be unbreathable for those poor pagans we continue to be.

I am not saying that there have not sometimes been practices that bordered on superstition. Yet I very intensely dispute whether a woman who is going to light a candle to our Lady when her baby is sick is performing a superstitious act, and I believe that in its humble form it is just as profoundly a religious act as more abstract prayers. I absolutely dispute whether an old lady who tells her beads in the rear of a church is doing something that is the residue of some kind of outdated mentality and I believe that she may well be more useful to society than the people who at the same time become overwrought during political rallies. We must not belittle all that the very simple, very true, very human forms of expression that come from the pagan soul represent. There were rosaries before the advent of Christianity: the old monks of India used them. Water was regarded as a sign of purification before the coming of Christianity. People climbed to mountain tops to pray before Christian times. I have often told the Carmelites that the high mountain to which they owe their name was first haunted by the priestesses of Astarte at the time of the Canaanite religions, before being used by pious Christian monks. In the final analysis, what does this mean?

It means that Christianity comes to reclaim everything without destroying anything, that Christ did not come to replace man by something else, but that he came to save the very man he had created. I think that the religious dimension of man is the noblest thing in him, and I fail to see how the Son of God, coming as he did to save man, could not have also saved that precious part of him — all the religious humanity, all that pagan humanity, all those basic religious attitudes. When I celebrate the feast of Easter, my thoughts revert to the fact that, behind the memorial of the resurrection of Jesus Christ, there is the memorial of the exodus of the Jewish people from Egypt at the time of the Mosaic religion and that, even prior to that, there is the memorial of the feast of springtime in the cosmic religion. Easter, then, for me, is not something scandalous but has something wonderful about it. Easter recapitulates in itself the whole of religious history; it recaptures the ancient religious actions of the pagans, the actions of the Jews in the Temple of Jerusalem, and brings all of this to an end in Jesus Christ, in whom all things end to ascend toward the Father.

In the Canon of the Mass, before the sacrifice of Jesus Christ, we commemorate the sacrifice of our father Abraham, and before the sacrifice of Abraham we commemorate the sacrifice of Melchisedech and of Abel who, to my knowledge, were not Jews, for the Jews were still non-existent in their days. These men are simply representatives of pagan mankind, witnesses of that cosmic religion which is the first way by which God was known to mankind. I do not call that compromising with conscience; I call it essentially incarnation. I mean that what constitutes the essence of Christianity for me is that the Word of God comes to recapture the whole man, just as he comes to recapture all men, and that, far from rejecting this human richness, he integrates it and assumes it in order to purify and transfigure it. This was also the basic and traditional attitude of the Church in regard to these pagan religions. Syncretism would have us put religions and Christianity on the same plane and in that way confuse things that have different, specific characteristics. It is my contention that we have to fend off such syncretism. Then too, when we bear in mind all that is human in the pagan soul, in that basic religion that is so deeply inserted in man, and when we delight in discovering this transfigured in our Christianity, we are defending a precious patrimony against all those present-day forces of secularization, of laicization, of desacralization that aim at affecting, within the faith itself, the religious substance of the human soul. Today we feel threatened even in our flesh. It is this basic religious experience that we have to defend against too many Christians who are susceptible to destructive ideologies. Let us not believe those false prophets who tell us that this is definitely condemned. It is definitely our duty to come to grips with the religious dimensions of the contemporary man. This man is as a whole no longer rural, but has now invented what will be the religious experience of urban civilization. But we must not believe that the man of urban civilization will not be capable of what the man of rural civilization was. And in our day, when we feel that something is awakening in the Church, is awakening in the Christian people, it is our duty to bring the revelation of Christ to new pagans, namely, to those men who are not atheists, but in whom there is an obscure search for God.

IV: The Content of Faith

We have tried to situate Christian revelation, the object proper of faith, with regard to the world of religion in general. We have pointed out at the same time that these basic religious values, common to all religions, were absolutely invaluable and sound, but that the Christian revelation put us in the presence of something quite different. It no longer was that obscure search for the absolute that arose from the depths of humanity down through the centuries, but God responding to that search, God coming to meet that humanity that was seeking him. We said that revelation was something that was not situated on the same plane as religion, as a general human fact, but that it should be considered as God's own response to that enormous question that humanity poses. It is obvious that this presents us with a more difficult problem than that posed for us by religion in general. As a matter of fact, we can say that the awareness of the mystery into which we are plunged, the experience gained by every man of the limitations of his power, and that obscure call toward a God who would come and free him, are all involved in forming part of man's experience. Surely, this can be tainted in many men of our age by a practical or speculative atheism, but nonetheless, every human heart is open to this experience.

On the other hand, it is much less obvious to affirm that God has come into the world, that the Son of God took flesh from a virgin of the lineage of Abraham, that this humanity with which he associated himself he has revived from the dead and lifted up into the sphere of the divine life, and that what was fulfilled in him continues in our midst through the sacraments of the Church. I would even go so far as to say that a priori it is unlikely. That God is God, is, we may say, as it should be. That God became man incontestably brings up quite different difficulties, entirely different objections. And that is why it is essential that we now take up what is, properly speaking, the object of our faith which, may I repeat, does not simply consist in a certain general belief in God. What is the basis of this faith in the heart of the twentieth century, in the face of this world with which we are confronted? How can we affirm to the intelligentsia of today the paradoxical statements that Christ is truly the Son of God made man, that he truly rose from the dead, and that he is truly present among us in the Eucharist, with the calm, firm, lucid and critical certitude which is the very condition of the intellect and therefore of witnessing to Jesus Christ in the fullness of what he is? We must admit that the question is a serious one: and it is undeniable that there is a great deal of uncertainty and confusion in this area in Christian circles, perhaps because priests themselves are uncertain and confused. It is certain that many Catholics today are asking themselves: "What must be believed?"

Faced with this lack of certitude, I would say that there are two equally dangerous attitudes. There is an attitude of fear which would make us look upon all the contributions of thought and of modern research, the progress of the sciences, as well as of the world of life and history, as menacing forces that threaten to shake the fragile edifice of our faith, because we tend to identify the very substance of our faith with certain forms that it happened to receive in the course of history. Now, our faith must be able to face the great blasts of the contemporary world. It must be a faith so vigorous that it does not need to surround itself with a whole set of defenses and supports without which we might fear that it would perish. What value would such a faith have for the youth of today? It would be a faith that would give the impression of being threatened on all sides. It would be simply a question of defending it against a hostile world.

The other danger is equally grave, and, in many respects, even more so. It is an impressionability regarding all the most uncertain and vaguest trends of modern thought, expressed in books in which the most contradictory opinions are defended. The result is that many end up saying to themselves: "After all, whether it be the virginal conception or the resurrection of Christ, are not all these statements of the faith merely secondary forms of expression and should we not be satisfied with a certain attachment to Christ without going into all the details of these problems?" A certain number of Christians today are therefore faced with the danger of a collapse of an authentic, doctrinal faith and all that is being kept of Christianity is a sort of morality, a gospel spirit of poverty and of charity. This question, then, must be deliberately faced in such a way that we are vindicated, whatever opinions we meet, in remaining rooted in our faith. Moreover, it is time for the Christian people themselves to affirm their faith in the face of those who are all too ready to destroy it or corrupt it.

And in this sense a basic, doctrinal firmness is one of the most important duties of today's Christians.

But theirs must be an enlightened faith. By that I mean a faith that is kept abreast of the research going on in the contemporary religious sciences, of exegesis, that science of Sacred Scripture, of theology, which is a reflection on the datum of revelation. This must be done if they are to deepen their faith in a way that does not equate the content of faith with certain forms of expression it has assumed. This will prevent their witness from being discredited by a deficient presentation. It is one thing to say, for example, that man was created by God and quite another thing to say that he was created by God from the dust of the earth. This latter statement in no way affects the substance of what my act of faith rests on, but merely concerns the manner in which creation was presented to men of an earlier time. I do not even refer to the assertion that the world was created in six days because obviously it would be ridiculous to interpret literally a distribution that derives from the Jewish week and from the Sabbath. We must distinguish between what is ascribable to the language of an era and what constitutes its essential content. There arises, then, the duty on the part of Christians today to be adequately well-read Christians. Now, there is a considerable discrepancy in many Christians between their secular culture, which is often very extensive, and their religious culture, which is simply content with statements received during their childhood. Not having taken into account an altogether very serious reflection by the Church, they themselves admit that they no longer distinguish between what constitutes the substance of their faith and what simply constitutes its forms of expression.

What, then, is the content of faith? As we already

The Content of Faith 69

said, there is in all mankind, and this is just as true of mankind today as it was yesterday, a basic question regarding the ultimate significance of his destiny. Whether men wish it or not, they are ultimately confronted with this mystery; even those who claim that they have found the last word for things in science or reason are still faced with the ultimate problems of existence, of responsibility, of love, and of death. "The gods," Maurice de Guérin said, "have buried the secret of the ultimate meaning of things somewhere, but where have they hidden the stone that hides it?" There is in fact a secret of the ultimate meaning of things which seems to be hidden to all men, which seems to escape their grasp. This is where Christian revelation comes in because it so happens that revelation is essentially the manifestation by God of the secret of the ultimate meaning of things, that is to say, of the meaning of our existence. That is what the Apostle Paul said when he presented his very own message to the Christians of Ephesus as the secret hidden in God from all eternity to call us to be his sons in Jesus Christ. He emphatically says: "This has been kept hidden in God" (Ep. 3,9). Moreover, a mystery for the Bible is not something incomprehensible, it is something that was kept secret before having been made known. And this secret directly concerns me. It is essentially the ultimate meaning of my destiny.

In an admirable text in the opening chapters of his Apocalypse, the Apostle John shows us a book sealed with seven seals which no one could open. Then, one of the elders said: "There is no need to cry: the Lion of the tribe of Judah, the Root of David . . . will open the scroll," and the text goes on to say: "then I saw . . . a Lamb that seemed to have been sacrificed" (Rv. 5, 5-6). In other words, the hidden content of the book, which only Christ unveils to us — that is what the word "revelation" means — is God's plan, is the immolated Lamb, Christ himself, to the extent in which we contemplate the man in him, such as God from all eternity willed to accomplish it and such as it is fully realized in him. To quote Pascal again: "Not only do we know God solely through Jesus Christ but we know ourselves only through Jesus Christ." Jesus Christ is the one who points to us the way to the mystery which we are to ourselves, for we know only too well that, whatever our introspections and our analyses, our psychologies and our psychoanalyses are, there is a final secret of what we are that completely escapes our grasp. God is not the only one who is a mystery to us. We are a mystery to ourselves, and what we are has to be revealed to us. It is precisely in Jesus Christ, in his humanity that we are shown what we are, that is to say, what is the nature of our condition in the plan of God, what is the final answer to all our questions, to all our questions regarding the final meaning of our destiny. And this meaning is that God wishes to make us living beings by having us share in his plentitude of life and existence.

If God, therefore, resolved to give life to this immense humanity down through the centuries, it was not in order that, after having called men to life for an instant, he might hurl them back into the nothingness from which they came. If this were so, then the history of mankind would be a sinister farce and I would join the atheists and would refuse to admit that one can attribute the fact of raising up hope in men and women to an intelligent and good God who then hurls them into the absurdity of death. What Christ reveals to us is that we are destined not to die but rather essentially to be living beings, that is to share a life that transcends the frontiers of what we call life and death, so that we might fully develop beyond that life in the mysterious fullness of God in which we will participate. There is a kind of paradox in this, a paradox, it seems to me, that we experience each day when we confront our faith with daily realities. There are times when we ask ourselves, "Are we not dreaming? Do these statements of ours truly apply to this poor humanity that loiters in our streets and loafs about in our trains, in our shops, seemingly unconcerned with so transcendent a destiny? And yet, this is true of every man and of every woman; it is true that every man and woman is the object of this infinite love of God who has sent his Son to give his life, even if for only one soul. Although they do not suspect it, all these souls, all these men, all these women have an infinite value in the eyes of God. They are more loved than they love themselves.

The paradox of our faith today lies in being confronted by a humanity so deeply involved in its material life that it gives the impression of being, as it were, a stranger to God, whereas we do know that the Holy Spirit is working within this sluggish humanity and does not grow weary in his effort. Our faith is contested, not only by intellectuals, but also by that sort of enormous indifference, of immense forgetfulness of God, by that terrible burden that we feel weighing down today on our world, a burden so great that at times we ask ourselves: "Shall we ever succeed in getting rid of it? Is it not this burden that little by little, despite every effort to the contrary, snuffs out all that the Holy Spirit tries to do in the depths of our heart?" But from the very beginning, from the first chapters of Genesis, we see Yahweh raise man up either from the dust of the ground or from an animal body, it matters little, and immediately lead him into paradise, that is, into a certain participation in the life of God. Scripture remains obscure about what primitive mankind was, and it is difficult to picture this first appearance. But of one thing we are sure, and it is this: as soon as there were men, they were called to share the life of God, they always had a supernatural destiny, and this destiny spans the totality of human history.

From the outset we see this destiny clashing with the denial of human freedom, and this original sin is transmitted to the rest of men. Henceforth there are two forces that oppose each other and each force will have its share in the story of our lives. On the one hand, there is a force of life, but of a life that is not simply biological life, of a life that is the life which the Spirit of God awakens in bodies and souls making men and women spiritual living beings. We are always coming back to the same idea: God wishes to make us living persons in the full sense of the word. And over against that, there is a force of death, which is not simply biological death but the deprivation of the life that the Spirit of God quickens in us, with the result that man is in a state of spiritual death. This evil is not composed solely of the bad desires of man, for, in that case, to make mankind happy and peaceable would ultimately depend on us. There is a root of evil that Scripture describes by means of such expressions as "the power of death," the "prince of this world," "Satan," whatever name by which we wish to designate it. It indicates the presence in creation of a force beyond man that resists God and of which man by himself is powerless to rid himself.

This vague destiny of mankind is, therefore, directed in a definitive way to the fullness of time by the decisive action of God who will come and take hold of the man he had created and who could not by himself succeed in attaining his destiny. God will do this in order to accomplish the destiny of human nature with which he became one. And Jesus Christ is that. He is — and that is why we dwell here on the fundamental objects of our

THE CONTENT OF FAITH 73

faith — not some kind of Galilean prophet who gave us some good instructions and good example. He is a man of our flesh; his mother is a woman of our race; he is, therefore, a man in the fullest sense of the word. That is why what was wrought in him was wrought in a flesh that is our flesh and consequently has its repercussions in our flesh. But Jesus Christ is at the same time that gesture of God's love coming into the world, that mission for which the Father in his love sent his Son. He is both — and this is his paradox — God-Savior and Man-Saved. The Old Testament did not foresee that; it did foretell that in the fullness of time there would be a decisive gesture on the part of God; it foretold that at the end of time a man would appear, but it did not understand that he would be the same one who will be the God who saves and the Man who is saved, a divine Person, made present in our world and flesh of man, assumed by it, saved and transfigured. Christ in this sense is both the God who has come to man and the man who ascends to God. Christ accomplished this in those basic mysteries which are the very object of our faith and which we enumerate when we profess our faith as we recite the Apostles' Creed.

"He was conceived by the Virgin Mary by the overshadowing of the Holy Spirit." I believe that, because it is of the very essence of my faith to believe that it is this race of Adam, which he had created from the beginning, that the Word of God came to seek in the fullness of time, and that it is truly this same humanity that was assumed by him. But at the time a new humanity begins with Jesus Christ, as St. Irenaeus admirably says: "Just as the first Adam had been formed by God from the virgin earth of paradise, so it was from the womb of a virgin that the new Adam was to be formed," in order to underscore that his flesh is our flesh, that he belongs to our race, and that, nevertheless, he inaugurated a new beginning of our race, that a new humanity is beginning. That is why there is in this mystery of the virginal Incarnation a creative work by God within the history of our race. And it has no common denominator, as I have heard it said, with the myths of the pagan religions in which the divinities of Olympus married goddesses. As a matter of fact, we cannot put the naturistic myths of the pagan religions on the same plane as the historical event whereby God who had created man in the beginning came and recreated him in the fullness of time. And that is why when you see the slightest doubt cast on the mystery of the virginal conception in any manual, in any article, or in any catechism, throw it away, for it assails what has always been one of the essential teachings of the faith of the Church: "He was conceived by the overshadowing of the Holy Spirit in the womb of the Virgin Mary." But we have to understand what that means. We must not look upon it as a somewhat strange marvel or the residue of some kind of reticence regarding the marriage act arising from a more or less Jansenistic mentality. We are, on the contrary, in the presence of an absolutely basic dogmatic statement, without which everything simply falls apart; for if Jesus Christ is not the bursting forth of this new humanity within our race, then he is just one more man among others, perhaps some prophet of the past, but no longer the saving act of God.

The body that the Word of God took in the womb of the Virgin Mary, he purified of its stain by his blood; in the mystery of the passion and of his descent into Sheol he confronted the forces of evil; and here we see again how the object of our faith concerns the very root of the human problem. How many times have I not heard it said: "Christianity is being called into question by

The Content of Faith 75

the very existence of evil and suffering." Now Christianity, the mystery of Christ, the mystery of the passion and resurrection of Christ, is the confrontation of evil, of suffering and of sin, not by way of some word of consolation or some philosophical explanation but in the only form in which it is permissible to speak in the face of suffering, death, and sin, that is, by destroying them. The resurrection of Christ marks the decisive confrontation of the strength of God with this mystery of evil which I spoke of just a minute ago. In the presence of this mystery all mankind is completely powerless, so much so, indeed, that in the end we can say that speeches are ridiculous, for what are speeches addressed to those condemned to death? Can anything be said in the face of suffering and death? Yes. But there is only one word that is acceptable at such times; the word of him who said: "I am the resurrection and the life. If anyone believes in me, even though he dies he will live" (Jn. 11,25). That is the basic statement of Christian faith. A short while ago we asked ourselves whether we have the right to take this statement seriously. We still have to show what it means and why it seems to be an answer to the question that all mankind is asking itself.

We are no longer on the plane of the daily routine of human stresses, on the plane of the medical battle against suffering and death or against misery or poverty in an effort to organize society, for in the happiest society and with the most efficient medications, we are still faced with certain limitations. Above all, there is the limitation of death. The problem consists in knowing whether a Christian has the right to have confidence in Christ when he says: "I am going so that I may prepare a place for you; have no fear of what lies beyond death; for that beyond, I have taken possession of; it is completely mine and when you step across the threshold, you will find him whom you have come to know very well." Christ has laid hold of all this somber world; he has completely conquered it and overcome it and we now know that we are no longer entering into some obscure and disquieting world, and still less than a nothingness that would swallow us up. We now know that he whom we will find and who will welcome us when we cross the threshold is he whom we have loved and served during our earthly life, the first to pass through this trial of suffering and death and to triumph over them; as a result, we can say with St. Paul: "Death, where is your victory" (1 Cor. 15,55).

The Word of God, having thus taken hold of our flesh, having quickened it by his resurrection, has ushered it into the life of God, into the house of his Father in order to unite himself to it in an eternal wedding. This wedding, so splendidly described in the Apocalypse, depicts the heavenly Church as a bride adorned for her Bridegroom. There is therefore part of our flesh that is already plunged into the abyss of divinity and transfigured by the vigor of the Spirit, which is already, according to the extraordinary imagery of St. Paul in the Epistle to the Hebrews, dropped like an anchor in the depths, not of the sea but of heaven (cf. Heb. 6,19). For it is true; our faith teaches that a part of our flesh, the part that Christ joined to himself, is already plunged into that life of God; and this is the guarantee that our poor flesh will one day be able to share this destiny. But already this humanity of Christ, the humanity that is ours, that humanity filled with the Holy Spirit, or what we call the Christ of glory, "seated at the right hand of God," becomes the source, the origin from which a force of life tends to spread itself over all flesh, by virtue of the connaturality of all flesh. That is what the Apocalypse describes for us when it shows us a river of living water, gushing from the throne of God and from the Lamb. This image describes for us the present moment of the divine history of humanity. For sacred history is not related only to the Old and New Testaments; it is the history of our present humanity in its mysterious depths. There is a living water in these mysterious depths, the very water which is the Spirit himself, who is at work, seeking to give birth to the life of the Spirit everywhere, to raise up living men everywhere or, as the Apostle John says, "trees of life" (Rv. 22,2). Those trees of life are all those who open themselves to the life of the Spirit.

We become living beings when we let this life invade us, when we abandon all the obstacles of our egoism, our pride, and our sensualities. This force of God fully enters into those who abandon themselves to it and makes great saints rise up in our midst. Who knows whether there are not in our times some such hidden saints, some of those outstanding living persons who constitute the greatest reality there is in the order of values. For, as Pascal said, the splendors of charity are infinitely greater than the splendors of the flesh or of the intellect. And woe to a Christianity that, as Maritain says, "kneels before the world." Woe to those Christians who become idolaters of carnal grandeurs, who let themselves be so impressed by the grandeurs of the intellect or by the grandeurs of power or of money that they forget that the genuine grandeurs are those of sanctity. Woe to a Christianity that loses its depths to that extent and becomes worldly by becoming an idolater of carnal grandeurs, whereas the distinctive characteristic of the spiritual man is to put things in their proper place and to know that what constitutes the greatness of a life is its spiritual success.

There will be surprises on judgment day, joyful surprises when we see so many visible facades collapse and discover where the true grandeurs really were, those hidden grandeurs that we were able to walk alongside of without suspecting them. It is this alignment of our judgment according to the light of faith instead of the spirit of the world that we have to bring about if we are to put ourselves again into reality, that is, into that which will blazon forth on the last day. This alignment of judgment is also necessary in order to discover that what is most essential is what the Spirit is trying to arouse in the heart of so many men and women, when he urges them to open themselves to his mysterious appeals, when he draws them to prayer, to charity, to humility, to genuine poverty, when he invites them to live in conformity to Jesus Christ. Surely this "fire of the Spirit," which Christ spoke of, when he said: "I have come to bring fire to the earth, and how I wish it were blazing already" (Lk. 12,49), and which seeks to set hearts afire with the life of Love, encounters an obstacle in those briar roots, unyielding as rock, which he does not succeed in touching and kindling because of the hardheartedness of our poor human hearts. One pities the Holy Spirit when one thinks of the enormous difficulty of his task. "Do not grieve the Holy Spirit of God" (Ep. 4,30) said St. Paul. What we are asked to do is to be his helpers in some small way, to take up his cause. To be an apostle means to work with the Spirit in raising up the life of the Spirit, to work at becoming living beings in order to help others to be living beings, to enter again into that immense stream of the life of God. What was accomplished in Jesus Christ was done only to be communicated to all mankind. That is why the present time is for us the time of extending to all mankind what was first accomplished substantially in the flesh of Christ.

I would like to say, by way of conclusion, that it is our

duty to discover how the object of our faith is in reality the answer to the vital problems which are not only our own but those of mankind around us. All too often the Christian dogmas of the Trinity, the Incarnation, and the Redemption (I sometimes regret this terminology in which words are in danger of concealing things) may seem more or less abstract truths that do not directly affect our life. We must discover that in reality these dogmas do affect the most profound, the most vital part of our lives, that is to say, the part of our existence which is not that superficial life whereby we let ourselves be taken in, but that deep-seated life from which we so often shy, yet where there is something which mysteriously attracts us to it. One of the earliest Fathers of the Church, Ignatius of Antioch, had this extraordinary saying: "There is a fountain of living water in me that murmurs: Come toward the Father." There is in every one of our souls a gushing fountain of living water. This fountain of living water came into our hearts at Baptism; it tries to re-awaken life in each one of us and to make us living beings. We must make an ever-greater response to the urging that it makes us hear. It is at that moment that we shall understand how all these basic tenets of our faith, which may seem paradoxical when we approach them from an external, extrinsic point of view, without grasping their meaning, seem to us, on the contrary, to correspond to something vital.

The object of faith is the plan of God's love for us. It shows us the authentic face of man in Jesus Christ, namely, what God seeks to carry out in man, what he seeks to carry out in each one of us, in such a way that we can say that Christian existence, and simply human existence, is in the end but a process of transformation into Jesus Christ. And everyone has to travel that road. There are those who have taken their first steps, to an extent, at least. And for those who have not done so, it will have to be done after death. It is in this sense that purgatory is for me one of the most evident mysteries of our faith, for when we see the way in which most poor men and women arrive at the threshold of death, and when we think that they are destined to contemplate the blessed Trinity for all eternity, we understand that they will need a serious moment of education, of purification, and of adaptation. Finally, to be a Christian is to have begun practicing in a very timid and very clumsy way what will be our eternal occupation, namely, the contemplation of divine things.

Through this plan of God, through his love for us, something of the end reveals itself, namely, what God is in himself. For in it is a proof of God the Father and Creator, a proof of Jesus Christ, a proof of the Spirit. This manifestation of God in the plan of his love leads us to discover that thing which is completely inaccessible without revelation and which no philosophy, no religion had ever suspected, namely, that God is from all eternity both one and three. What this means is that love is contemporaneous with being, that is to say, that the very structure of the absolute is love, that the last abyss, when we go beyond all appearances, when we see all the veils rent asunder, is not matter, not nothingness, not relative, but eternal love which is constitutive of the absolute itself. We understand that if the absolute itself is love, if he manifested this love by calling us into existence in order to share his life and if in the final analysis he invites us to love one another, the whole object of our faith is finally reduced to these three simple truths: God is eternally Love, God loved us, and we must love one another. But to say that we must love one another takes on a singularly greater resonance when we know that the love with which we are to love one another is

The Content of Faith 81

a participation in Love itself with which God has loved us and ultimately in the eternal love which is the bond of the three divine Persons. This is the vision that is ours. This is the exalting object of our faith. This is the Good News of the gospel that we must still shout today to the whole world.

V: The Foundations of Faith

We have tried to isolate what constitutes the very substance of faith from a certain matrix in which it is inevitably imbedded by reason of the fact that this faith is transmitted to us through the books of the Old or New Testament, then through a historical tradition in which, of course, truths which are permanent are conveyed by way of the successive forms of the different cultures through which they have traveled. And this is essential, for our duty is to transmit to our times the faith in its substance, striving to express it in the language of the men of today. What constitutes the essence of our faith is the revelation of the mystery of what God is and of what we are. This revelation enables us to go beyond what all the sciences, all the introspections, all the philosophies can attain since we also know that all these methods of investigation finally end in an enigma. The object of faith is to cause us to reach this last enigma, this last mystery which is inaccessible to our own intellects. Our faith deals with the successive stages by which God carried out his plan, paving the way for it in the Old Testament, fulfilling it in the mysteries of Christ, his virginal incarnation, his passion and resurrection, his ascension, continuing it in the Church where, since Pentecost, the outpoured Spirit is at work through the sacraments in the hearts of believers. It is this total vision of the ensemble of God's plan that is the object of our faith.

In view of the wonderful unfolding of God's plan, a question is bound to be asked and must be asked. Is not all this an unquestionable creation of our desire for happiness? Does all this have for us men and women of the twentieth century a true, objective basis that gives us the right to commit our lives and our intellects to the word of Christ and of the Church? The question is a serious one, for if faith is truly a genuine faith, it binds our whole intellect and our whole life to this revelation; it is also serious to the extent that once we know it to be true, we have not only the right but the duty to bear witness to it before others and to urge of them that adhesion of the intellect which is owed to all truth. Now, it is certain that we often feel bankrupt when we are confronted with objections, with contradictions, or with the reticences of this or that believer. We even hear these objections in our own circles, from members of our own families and from our friends. A certain number of problems are raised and they must be answered.

There is, first of all, a preliminary question which has no bearing on the substance of the question but which is nonetheless important. From the simple viewpoint of history, what value is there in those documents by which we are placed in contact with the events of the ancient history of the People of God and especially with the events which concern Christ? We very often come across ideas on this subject that are somewhat confusing to the minds of some people. If we ask certain people whether Jesus Christ is truly a historical person or instead a somewhat mythical figure, many are really not sure. But we must go even farther. The historicity, in the very simple and commonplace meaning of the word, of the events of the Old and especially of the New Testament, has been and still is contested in our time by a number of exegetes and critics. A great deal has been said during these recent years about Rudolph Bultmann, one of the most important contemporary German Protestant exegetes. He founded *the School of the history of forms*. In this school it is claimed that the narratives of the infancy of Christ, of his public life and his miracles, of his resurrection, his appearances, are actually literary devices that are not based on historical reality properly so-called. When all is said and done, we know precious little about Jesus, except that he lived and that the community he founded, built up a certain number of legends around his childhood, his life and his death. We feel obligated to allude to this teaching, because these ideas are being circulated today in a number of books and they upset many people.

It is very important to say here that, on the strictly scientific level, these challenges concerning the historicity of the life of Christ as it is reported in the gospels are without foundation. Certainly, and this is clear enough, the gospels are not biographies in the sense in which a modern historian sets out to write a biography of Napoleon or of Churchill, that is, by looking up all the details available which can provide information on the events of his life. This was not the intention of the authors who wrote the gospels. The aim of the evangelists was to present Christ to the men of their time, in such a way as to emphasize the interesting points of his life and teaching from the viewpoint of faith. Consequently they did not linger over details, such as physical descriptions, exact chronologies, or descriptions of the places where Jesus lived. But we can say that the gospels are essentially the utilization of a datum which is substantially and basically historical, with an eye to preaching and teaching.

Here I shall stress three points very briefly. First, during the past thirty years we have rediscovered what we were almost ignorant of, namely, the historical and geographical context of the life of Jesus, the Jewish milieu in which his destiny unfolded. We owe this to one of the most extraordinary discoveries of modern times, that of the Dead Sea scrolls from the library of a Jewish community contemporary with Christ, which incontestably describes striking resemblances with the milieu in which Jesus recruited his disciples. This is an important link: we are finding out more and more that Jesus' life unfolded not in some ideal world, not in some Palestine outside of time, not in some more or less Eden-like region, but in a country that was politically in a state of revolution and subversion. The Palestine in which Jesus lived was a land occupied by the Romans, who were not only foreigners but pagans, and this occupation by pagans brought about varied types of reactions among the Jewish people. There were the Sadducees who collaborated with the occupying forces. There were the advocates of violent revolt, the underground resistance of the time, who went by the name of Zealots. There were the non-violent resistants, the Essenes, who awaited the deliverance of the people from God alone. All of this re-situates the life of Jesus in a context singularly close to that of contemporary events. These discoveries help us to realize that the life of Jesus took place in the circumstances of a humanity absolutely similar to ours. Such circumstances are highly interesting because they link the context of Jesus' life to a human context.

THE FOUNDATIONS OF FAITH   87

As for the person of Jesus himself and the events of his life, how are we sure that we have direct access to them? I shall limit myself to three brief remarks. As for the events of Jesus' public life, we know them through the apostles who had been eyewitnesses to them. In this, then, we have a classical witness of an absolutely incontestable historicity. Objections are very often raised about the infancy narratives. Are they not narratives of a legendary nature? There is no reason to think so. Certainly, the presentation of one or the other of these episodes, as well as of those of Jesus' public life, can have received a certain stylization from the gospel writers, with the intention of highlighting some particular detail. I am thinking, for example, of the story of the Magi. But even here there is no room to dispute whether it corresponds to a historical fact. On the contrary, there is something quite extraordinary about the narrative. Two horoscopes of the Messiah were recently found at Qumran in the Dead Sea scrolls. This points to the fact that the Jews of that time were preoccupied with determining under what star the Messiah would be born. The story of the Magi, which may seem to be completely extraordinary to us, corresponds, therefore, to a specific characteristic of the mores of the times.

While we are on the subject of the infancy narratives, I might add that there is another detail about Christian origins that up to now has not been stressed, and this is the extraordinary position held by Jesus' family, his cousins, male and female, his uncles and aunts, in the primitive Christian community. It is a historical fact that all the first bishops of Jerusalem were cousins of the Lord. Exactly the same thing happened seven centuries later for Mohammed. In a Semitic milieu, the tribe seeks to make the most of the success of one of its members. This has the tremendous advantage of putting us in the human reality of the world of Christian origins: a world in which divine things are carried out but where these divine things are accomplished in a human context. Such continues to be the case. The Christian paradox consists precisely in the fact that the divine is accomplished in the very midst of the human and of the most banal human at that. They are the same people who with a part of themselves belong to daily life in all its banality and who at the same time receive the risen Christ into their hearts in Holy Communion. Christianity is not something that is situated halfway between the world of God and the world of man. Christianity is, on the contrary, both divine truth and human truth, the presence of God within this poor humanity of ours. There is not one myth in the entire gospel, just as there is no myth in the entire Church. But God is acting and present within human reality. Now, the advantage of knowing the role that this whole tribe of Jesus played during the first centuries of Christianity lies in showing us that, when the gospels were written, there were people who were witnesses not only of the events of Jesus' public life but also of the events of his childhood. Furthermore, in view of these living witnesses, it is completely incomprehensible that legends could have been concocted. Such a thing would be the very negation of the historical method as such.

To say categorically that we cannot know the historical reality of the life of Christ is scientifically debatable. Consequently, we can recapture the joyful certitude that we have historically valid data in the gospels, and we have every right to tell children the story of the Magi, the story of Bethlehem, the story of the Presentation in the Temple, the story of the public life of Christ, the story of the passion, the story of the resurrection, the story of the appearances of Jesus to his disciples, and the story of his ascension to the right hand of the Father, as historical truths. These are things that must be said publicly, for if we were to read certain articles we would end up being persuaded to the contrary. Now, from the point of view of exegesis, we have not the slightest justification for calling into question the substantial historical value of all these episodes in the life of Jesus.

There is another question that is raised. Do the gospels transmit to us the authentic sayings of Jesus? It is certain, for example, that in St. John's Gospel the teaching of Jesus seems to us to have been expanded by the gospel author. But as for the body of Jesus' teachings, in particular in the Synoptics, one of the points emphasized by contemporary exegesis is that what characterized the civilization of that time was the fact that it was a civilization of oral style. A rabbi was essentially one who made his disciples learn from memory. Even today in a Koranic school, the children have to memorize the Koran. That is exactly what the rabbis of Jesus' time did. Christ's teaching consisted essentially in having his disciples memorize things that they did not understand. This explains why our Lord is constantly saying in the gospel to his disciples: "But when will you understand?" It also explains Christ's words before ascending to the Father: "the Advocate, the Holy Spirit . . . will teach you everything and remind you of all I have said to you" (Jn. 14,26). As a matter of fact, the Apostles understood what they had learned only when the Holy Spirit was given to them, for as long as the Holy Spirit had not been sent to them, they could not understand. All they could do was learn. Now, everyone knows that there is a guarantee of authenticity when someone repeats something he does not understand, for the person who understands runs the risk of injecting his own personal interpretation into it. I have stressed these points because, if it is essential to believe that Christ is the Son of God, it is equally essential to our faith that Christ be a true man, a man who has truly lived. For if the Word has not truly assumed our humanity, he has not saved our humanity. "One saves only what he has assumed," according to an axiom of the ancient theologians. And this reality of the humanity of Christ, this reality of the historical Christ, is one of the two constitutive elements of our faith.

The great difficulty does not lie in believing that there was a man named Jesus who preached love of neighbor and practiced poverty. It consists in believing that this man is God who came among us. This is what constitutes the act of faith properly speaking. Many men love Jesus and yet do not believe in him. I will even go farther and say: almost all men love Jesus. What I mean is that there are few men, whatever religion or irreligion they may claim, who do not respect Jesus. I am thinking especially of the Jews whose position in regard to Jesus has reversed itself in the last twenty years. I am thinking of Edmund Fleg, the great Jewish poet and friend of Péguy, who wrote "Jesus vu par le juif errant"; of Robert Aron, who has just published *Les années obscures de Jésus,* of David Flusser, a professor at the University of Jerusalem. They deeply admire and love Jesus, but they do not believe that he is the Son of God.

This is also true of the Moslems. Jesus, Isha, occupies an eminent place in the Koran. Mohammed considered him the greatest of all the prophets. Likewise the mother of Jesus, Miriam, is venerated by the Moslems. They believe in the virginal motherhood. And so Moslems share our veneration for Jesus and Mary, although they do not believe that Jesus is the Son of God. The Hindus have a great veneration for Jesus. Ramakrishna, the Hindu mystic of the latter part of the nineteenth century, ranked Jesus among the great leaders, and we know what an enormous influence the gospel had on Gandhi, the great Indian prophet of non-violence. He admitted that his teaching came in very great part from the gospel. Many atheists venerate Jesus as representing one of the highest summits of generosity and self-sacrifice. Fifty years ago Henri Barbusse wrote a life of Jesus in which he portrayed him as the foremost revolutionary agitator. We might take exception to this interpretation, but it vouches for the deep respect Barbusse had for Jesus whom he considered to be the first one to come to the defense of the poor. And many non-believers take the same stance. Jesus, in his humanity, is respected by almost all of mankind. But it is not enough to love Jesus, we must also believe in him. We must make the transition from a human love of him to divine faith in the incarnate word. And we have to examine ourselves and ask ourselves whether our love of Jesus is not basically more an attachment to his human image with all the idealism of his poverty, humility, and charity than a true faith in Jesus, the Son of God who came into the world to save us.

This is a paradoxical statement which at first glance gives rise to incredulity. In this regard the model of the believer is not the man who pounces on these statements with a sort of avidity because they correspond to some kind of need of his and to some kind of attraction, but rather the incredulous Thomas who said: "I'll believe it when I see it," and whose normal reaction is that of a critical mind. That is why it is good and indispensable that our faith be not simply a sort of impulse, even though legitimate. But we still need to assume and develop our faith in the divinity of Jesus in a precise way, yes, I would even say in a critical way. The faith of a twentieth century Christian must be an enlightened faith, a faith that can subject its tenets to the testing fire of criticism and verify whether these beliefs come through unscathed, for there is nothing more demoralizing than the impression that we are coldly defending some more or less fragile edifice in the fear that with the first gust of wind it will crumble to the ground. Our faith must be tested by storms, by intellectual and social disturbances. Genuine faith is that faith which no ideology has succeeded in calling into question or in shaking its foundations down through the centuries. There is no reason why the faith should be any weaker today than it was ten centuries ago, for there is nothing in our modern ideologies that should rightly shake our faith in the divinity of Christ. In fact, in some respects these modern ideologies are less cogent than certain more formidable ideologies of the nineteenth century. Now, what is the basis of our faith?

The first foundation is words of Christ, or what the gospels tell us of Christ. But we must always be on our guard when it comes to the words of Christ because they are often ambiguous. When a text says that Jesus is the Son of God, the phrase in itself is not decisive, because in the Old Testament the Jewish people are called sons of God and we are also told that we ourselves are sons of God. Therefore an expression such as that is not conclusive. On the other hand, we must be careful of words for another reason: we can ask ourselves whether this or that expression was introduced only at a later date. There is certainly such a thing as the history of the texts and we may ask whether such and such an expression truly forms part of the primitive and original content. Hence we shall not speak first of all of the words but of things. We must begin with things; things are solid and the only value of words lies ultimately in their reference to things. We are not one of those who believes that language is constitutive of reality. We believe that reality is what gives meaning to language and what interests us is not words but things. Words are merely tools for expressing things and what interests us are the realities signified by the words.

In the matter at hand, what is the essential known quantity? It is Christ's ways of acting as found throughout the gospel, a matter of the very fabric of what constitutes the totality of Christ's life, which contains a proof within itself. Now, when we examine all Christ's behavior, one absolutely certain conclusion emerges. And here I weigh all my words very carefully and limit myself to what offers an unquestionable proof. There is something that offers an unquestionable proof and it is this: Christ acted as one having an authority, a power, a dignity of a divine order. I am not yet saying that Christ had the right to do so. That will be a second step. But I do say that we have there something which is a scientific certitude. In other words, the image of Jesus as a simple prophet who spoke of God, who preached doing good, has nothing to do with the authentic Christ of the gospel. The authentic Jesus acted as God. I shall give some examples of this. After curing the paralytic, Jesus said to him: "Your sins are forgiven you." Some Pharisees were present and they made this significant remark: "Who is this man talking blasphemy? Who can forgive sins but God alone?" (Lk. 5,20ff) What attitude do the Pharisees adopt? They note that Jesus acknowledges that he has the power to forgive sins; they know that only God forgives sins; but, since they do not believe that Jesus Christ is God, they consider him a blasphemer. But for us the advantage of the narrative lies in the fact of their witness that Jesus did forgive sins and in that sense admitted that he possessed a divine power properly so-called. Having admitted this, were the Pharisees correct in seeing in Jesus' claim to have this power a blasphemous appropriation? Or are we the ones who are correct when we say that he had the right to act that way? We shall discuss this further on. For the time being, I am simply citing the facts.

In the Sermon on the Mount Jesus said: "You have learnt how it was said: Eye for eye and tooth for tooth . . . But I say this to you: love your enemies and pray for those who persecute you" (Mt. 5, 38-45). Who had said: eye for eye and tooth for tooth, that is, who issued that law? Yahweh on Sinai. Therefore, when Jesus said: "You have learnt . . ., but I say this to you," he puts his authority on a par with the authority of the one who had issued the law. And this is so true that a few years ago a rabbi made this remark to me in the course of a discussion we were having; the remark is exceptionally interesting because it shows that the attitude of the Jews of today in regard to Jesus remains ever the same: "Father, there is one thing we cannot forgive Jesus for, and it is this: he modified the Law; now, the Law had been given by God and God alone can change what has been laid down by God." My answer was: "Rabbi, you could not say anything that could give me greater pleasure! For I perfectly agree with your first remarks: the Law was drawn up by God; God alone can change what he set down. It is clear, moreover, that Jesus did modify the law. Therefore, the question that separates us is precisely this one: Did he have the right to do so?" It is obvious that, on the very admission of this rabbi, only God could change the law; therefore when Jesus modifies the law, he actually does something that is reserved to God alone. The discussion always revolves around the second proposition. Did Jesus have the right or not to change the law?

There is a third and most important example of all. At the time of his trial, witnesses were sought who would testify against Jesus. The trial was a perfectly legal one. There was a certain number of witnesses but their testimony did not seem to be valid. It was at this point, the gospels tell us, that a witness came forth and stated: "This man said, 'I have power to destroy the Temple of God and in three days build it up . . .' At this, the high priest tore his clothes" and made the accusation we heard before: 'He has blasphemed. What need of witnesses have we now' . . . They answered; 'He deserves to die' " (Mt. 26, 61-66). What did that mysterious testimony mean? To a Jew it was all too clear. The Temple for a Jew was the place where God dwelt. To say therefore — and this is exactly the meaning of what Christ said —: You can destroy the Temple of Jerusalem, because Yahweh no longer dwells in a temple of stones, he dwells in me. In other words, to say: "Destroy the Temple, and I shall rebuild it," was the same as saying: "I am the equal of the Temple." It is obvious that, in making himself the equal of the Temple, he was making himself the equal of God. And this always elicits from the Jews the same accusation that runs through the entire gospel: the accusation of blasphemy.

Now, this accusation is in itself legitimate. The greatness of the Jewish nation lies, as a matter of fact, in condemning every aspiration by man to make himself God. For the Jews there was no worse sin than to attribute divine power to oneself, to divinize oneself: it was idolatry. The only question that remains to be solved is whether in one case and in one case alone, there was not a man who had the right to call himself God, because, as a matter of fact, he was God. That is the whole problem that separates Jews from Christians insofar as the person of Jesus is concerned. But it is obvious that insofar as the Jews did not believe that Jesus was God, they had to condemn him to death as a blasphemer; and we can say that the drama of the Jews is that confronted with Jesus they had no other choice than to believe in him or to condemn him, for there is no other Jesus than the Jesus who laid claim to a divine dignity. Now, in regard to this Jesus, a Jew cannot be neutral: a man who lays claim to a divine dignity is either a blasphemer who deserves death or else he is truly God and he must be believed in. This is what happened at the time. There were Jews who condemned Jesus as a blasphemer and there were Jews who acknowledged that he was the Savior of the world.

In the last analysis that is what the problem reduces itself to, and the option is final. It is clear that Jesus laid claim to a divine dignity: this is a scientifically established fact and admitted by all. Either he is God or he is not. If he is not, then he is an impostor, someone who palmed himself off as God. There have been a few such impostors in the history of mankind but they have all ended up by being hated and ridiculed. Or at best, he was a visionary, a harmless dreamer who let himself be taken in by some myth. But this is impossible in virtue of what we have already said: All men, even atheists agree that Jesus is one of those men whom the human race honors most. We should not forget that just a short while ago we saw that there is a quasi-unanimity on this point. I do not know a single man who would say: Jesus is an impostor or a visionary. We cannot say, as all men from Fleg to Gandhi, from Barbusse to Jeanson do, that at very least Jesus is a person who by his poise, his uprightness, and his self-sacrifice is an honor to humanity and at the same time say that this same man is a mental case, an impostor, or a visionary. That is impossible, for it is contradictory. We must, therefore, say that the problem of the divinity of Jesus is a problem that is raised in the most serious and most exacting way intellectually, for it is, as a matter of fact, the answer that best fits all these data. And, of course, confronted with this answer our intellect hesitates, for it involves us to a tremendous degree. But the whole problem of Jesus is this: is not the impossible the truth? In other words, by what right do the limitations of our intellects and of our concepts obstruct the freedom of God's love from carrying out its designs? In the end Jesus Christ is the freedom of a love that is not a prisoner of human categories within which we would enclose it. What right have we to say that the marvel that Jesus Christ represents, that the Good News that the gospel represents, that the splendor of the resurrection could not be the truth?

But this intervention of God in Jesus Christ in the New Testament is not an isolated event. It stands out as being not something peculiar and altogether exceptional, as without any reference to other facts, but as the summit and decisive moment of a history that had already begun and was to continue. One mysterious sentence recurs quite frequently in the New Testament: "Now all this took place to fulfill the words spoken by the Lord through the prophet" (Mt. 1,22). In other words, when Christ himself wanted to provide evidence for his disciples to help them believe the unlikelihood of his resurrection, "starting with Moses and going through all the prophets, he explained to them the passages throughout the scriptures that were about himself" (Lk. 24,27). If there is one time in the gospel when I would have loved to have been there, it is this one, for I would have been interested in knowing what Scripture texts Christ commented on for his disciples on that occasion.

Here we see Christ bolstering the faith of his apostles

and showing them that what was accomplished in him represents the highest form of something which had already been begun in an imperfect manner, that is, God had already intervened in human history and the events of his resurrection and ascension were but the summit of this intervention. Even on the threshold of the gospel, when the angel Gabriel — who in this sense ought to be the patron of all catechists — wished to help the Blessed Virgin make an act of faith in the unlikely thing he was announcing to her, that the Holy Spirit would overshadow her and that the One to be born of her would be called the Son of the Most High, he gave her a proof. And this proof was the birth of John the Baptist, son of her cousin Elizabeth who was sterile. This would show Mary that what was about to be accomplished in her represented a divine action of a much greater scope indeed, but which ultimately was consistent with the way in which the living God acted. Likewise, the fact that during the paschal night the power of God had snatched the humanity of Jesus from death was a reminder that on that same paschal night the power of God had liberated the people of Israel from a hopeless situation when, brought to a standstill by the sea and doomed to extermination, they were delivered by the power of God alone. There is a holy history, a history of salvation, a divine history. The events fulfilled in Jesus Christ are not isolated events; they represent the supreme moment of something that began with the origins of the world, with the ushering of man into paradise, and that continue on in our midst through the sacraments, which are the continuation in the lifetime of the Church of the wondrous deeds of God in the Old and New Testaments. We are always living in sacred history. The resurrection of Christ is not an isolated fact. The departure from Egypt was already an act of liberation and baptism is still an act

THE FOUNDATIONS OF FAITH 99

of liberation.

What then, by way of conclusion, is faith? It is believing that there are divine actions in our world which constitute the divine history of humanity. There are divine ways of acting that are met with in the Old Testament, in the New Testament, and in the Church. Faith, therefore, reduces itself to an extremely simple content. It consists in believing that God creates, that is to say, that he is capable of raising up something where there was nothing and of entirely renewing what was old or dead. It consists in believing that God saves, that is, that there are situations totally hopeless, from the human point of view, from which the power of God alone is capable of liberating man. It consists in believing that God makes a covenant, that is, he enables those whom he wishes to share in his gifts: the sacrament of that covenant in the Old Testament was the paschal lamb; in the New Testament it is "the blood of the new covenant." It consists in believing that God judges, discerns good from evil and on the last day will manifest what is truth, whereas all that is a lie will appear in its nothingness. Then, when we see that this already explains all the history that precedes Christ and continues to do so down through history, there is a certain dimension and depth to all history, something that in itself carries such massive evidence that it justifies my adhesion. To believe is precisely to believe that this totality is something profoundly and absolutely real and that to bear witness to it is simply to have one's eyes open to the reality of things.

This is the history that is continuing in the Church to which Christ, before ascending to his Father, entrusted the treasures of his truth and of his holiness. And that is why the Church, which is poor, to the extent that she is composed of poor men and poor women, to the extent that she possesses nothing of her own, is nevertheless for us richer than the richest of the rich, to the extent that she possesses the incomparable treasures that Christ, her Bridegroom, gave her. This is the meaning of the nuptial mystery of the eternal wedding of Christ and of the Church: the real gift and the sharing that Christ gave her of all that he has, namely, his infallible truth and his quickening holiness. That is why in these days of uncertainty, of dispute, of questioning, there is something we cannot question, we cannot contest, that cannot be shaken, because this something does not depend on human authority. It is part of our belief that the Church is assisted by the Holy Spirit and that this Holy Spirit sees to it that her teaching remains infallible and is not at the mercy of the fluctuations of opinions and that, although she includes many sinful men, she continues in her sacraments to be the source of that holiness which makes us living spiritual beings.

VI: The Growth of Faith

There is, on the one hand, an element of permanence in faith, that is, what was said in Jesus Christ was said once and for all and nothing of it can be changed. And what is even more paradoxical in a sense — in Jesus Christ who is God's Word, God has said all that there is to say. Nothing will ever be added to what has been said in Jesus Christ. In Jesus Christ God has unveiled to us the fullness of all that we need to know regarding the mystery of God and the mystery of our existence. We have already said this, and it is one of the paradoxes of the Christian position. There is nothing beyond Jesus Christ; the in-break of God into history which took place two thousand years ago is the decisive and final event beyond which nothing further can be added. The idea, for example, that Jesus Christ could have simply represented a period in the history of religions that would be destined to be replaced by another religion (in other words, that after the Christian religion there would be a new religion which in turn would give way to another), make no sense whatsoever, because in Jesus Christ the last word has been said. He is the Word, he is the utterance, he is the definitive expression of all that we need to know about God and about ourselves. Anyone who would attempt to meddle with this immutable block of faith would affect the very substance of Christianity. Consequently it is our right and duty to resist everything that would question either the content of faith or the permanence of the institution as Christ established them and which no man has the power to modify. Cardinal Marty expressed this very well: "The faith is something whose deposit we must watch over; we are its servants. It is not something that belongs to us which we may dispose of at will." The faith is not a reality that we have the right to change as we please. It is our absolute duty to protest against any alteration of that to which we have rightly committed our life.

On the other hand, this does not in the least mean that the Christian attitude is a fixed, set, ultra-conservative attitude. The datum of faith is immutable in its content, but our understanding of it is something that can grow indefinitely. And we may say that therein lies the magnificent adventure of the Christian intellect. There is no denying the fact that if the faith suppressed every desire of research, it would run counter to the deepest aspirations of the contemporary mind. But faith puts no limitations on research; instead, faith adds a domain to research, that is, it enlarges the dimensions of reality and this results in the fact that our field of exploration is infinitely more vast than that of an intellect whose knowledge would be restricted to the material cosmos. If I take the material world and science as an example, I do so because this analogy is basic. Scientific research is not a challenge of reality. Scientific research does not absolutely test the existence of things. Physics presupposes the existence of a certain number of phenomena.

It basically consists in trying to fathom the nature of these phenomena. Astronomy implies the reality of the planetary and stellar universe. It also consists in making a progressive inventory of this universe; it is in a way a progressive discovery of reality, and that is precisely the noble function of the intellect. But today we have another conception of the intellect, which sees it not as plumbing reality but as contesting it. Now, this aspect of the intellect is doomed to sterility, for it is all too obvious that as soon as we contest the existence of things we destroy reality and, instead of furthering research, we deprive it of the enormous domains which it needs if it is to develop.

What, then, in this sense is theology? Theology consists in a never-ending exploration of that reality which was given once and for all, namely, Jesus Christ. For Christ has been given to us once and for all. Yet we will never succeed in exhausting the plentitude of Jesus Christ, for his plentitude is something greater than the totality of the universe. Jesus Christ is himself a universe greater than the universe. We shall never reach the frontiers of Jesus Christ. He opens up for us a new dimension of life. And just as science will never exhaust the content of the material universe, so will we never succeed in exhausting the immensity of Jesus Christ. And therein lies the prodigious adventure of the Christian intellect, of constantly striving to reach an ever-greater understanding of what was given once and for all. What would we add to Jesus Christ? Jesus Christ transcends everything that we could invent. But our intellect will never cease fathoming ever more and more the inexhaustible reality of the mystery of Christ. And that is where the basic antinomy, the antinomy of the union of the permanent and forward movements, of immutability and of perpetual movement, will be resolved.

An incorrect concept of immutability would attempt to freeze not only the datum of faith but the understanding of faith. Does this mean that all we can do is go on and on repeating what our predecessors have said? Would not the intellect simply add useless things to what had already been said once and for all? It is clear that there can be a too rigid conception of immutability in theology, in liturgy, in all domains. But this conception does not correspond to the vitality of the presence of the Holy Spirit within the Church who, in the immutability of what is abiding, is constantly a source of discovery.

On the other hand, obviously, an attitude that would consist, not in making headway into the interior of what has been given once and for all, but in contesting what is given once and for all, would be false because it would affect the very substance of what has been acquired once and for all. Surely, we will never exhaust what is meant by saying that Christ rose from the dead. To say that Christ is risen is to say something which is so great that our understanding of it will always have to grow. But the moment that we contest the reality of the resurrection of Jesus Christ, we are no longer engaged in research, in the genuine sense of the word; but in a rejection of reality. There is one thing that we ought never to admit, namely, that we question what is constitutive of what Jesus Christ instituted, fulfilled, and revealed. It is in this sense that there is a fidelity to the integrity of the faith which is essential, but it is equally true that we must advance in our understanding of the reality that faith reveals to us. That is where theological research, as the endeavor of one who has the faith to understand what he believes, finds its full justification. St. Anselm expressed the same idea succinctly: "Fides quaerens intellectum," faith seeking to understand better that which it believes. Faith already overtakes the substance of things in a definitive way. We will have to await eternal life in order to truly understand all we have believed. Nevertheless, as of now, it is our duty to strive to better understand this datum which has been proposed to us once and for all and within which we always have to advance.

This synthesis of permanence and research is important to understand. For there are minds that reject the faith because they fear that it puts an end to research and that from the moment one has the faith there is nothing left to search for because one has an answer to everything. Indeed, we do have the definitive answer, but we must strive to understand that definitive answer, and that is where research regains all its rights. The Christian attitude is not a kind of immobilism calling for no more progress and development, but a progress and a development within a basic fidelity. What is true of these abstruse endeavors that we engage in during this present life in order to understand our faith better will continue throughout eternity, which will eternally consist in this sort of synthesis of possession and research. For even during eternity, henceforth rooted unshakeably in the beatific vision, we will nevertheless forge ahead in the discovery of this God whose frontiers will always transcend what we will be able to attain of them. It will always remain a marvel, every day will reveal to us a new aspect of it, but we will never succeed in exhausting its fullness. Paradise will consist in going from one amazement to another, that is to say, it will be an inexhaustible discovery of the unfathomable abyss of God.

This growth within faith depends on theology, but also on mysticism. Mysticism is a quest of the soul seeking to encounter the divine absolute. It is a basic dimension of human existence which we meet in all religions. From this point of view, the search for God is not a Christian fact properly so-called. We can even say from this point of view that there are civilizations in the world that can teach Western civilization something. While we Occidentals are preoccupied with making an inventory of the material and external world in order to put it at our beck and call, the tradition of India, in particular, has been more preoccupied with making an inventory of the interior world to see how man could succeed in progressively uncovering its hidden depths. In Indian spirituality, in yoga, in all that results from these quests of inner experience, there is something that expresses a dimension of humanism contrary to that of the mastery of the material world, but which we definitely feel corresponds to a profound and unsatisfied need. In the world of our times the interior life is atrociously tread upon; it is, as it were, rendered incapable of exercising itself because of the frightful burden of our material occupations. Mysticism is that thirst, inherent in the heart of every man, for a certain union with the absolute. But it cannot be separated from truth. If that mysticism is not an encounter with the living God as he reveals himself in Jesus Christ, if it is not the interior aspect of that of which Christ is the objective content, then we know how that mysticism can go astray, can lose itself. This is what happens very often to certain oriental mysticisms which attract souls who are reaching out for an inner equilibrium but fail because they are not grounded in the light of truth. Intellectual adhesion to truth and the interior experience of life must be joined together at one and the same time, for they are inseparable.

The temptation of the man of today, as we said in the beginning, is to attach importance only to interior experience and to make the faith something purely subjective. This we absolutely reject. Faith is not primarily a question of inner experience; faith is first of all a question of truth. The problem does not consist in knowing what I feel; it consists first of all in knowing who exists. It is a question of knowing first of all whether God exists and only then does the experience I can have of God have a meaning. But all the experiences that I may undergo, to the extent that they are not brought into contact with truth, are in the end questionable and susceptible of multiple psychological, sociological, and other interpretations. It is, therefore, essential to know whether God exists. It is essential to know whether Christ is truly the Son of God who has come into this world. From this viewpoint, objective truth is the point of departure of everything. If Christ has not risen from the dead, any and all experiences that I may go through have not the slightest importance. Therefore, it is essential that the certitudes of faith be well-grounded. But on the other hand, since Christ is risen, it is essential that the risen Christ be for me not simply an abstract truth but the living encounter of him who is a living Person. In other words, faith must become life to the extent to which it is an adhesion of the intellect, in the sense in which it is the personal encounter of a living God.

In this world of today in which the interior dimension of man is so neglected, in which we are in special danger of becoming victims of activism in one form or other, even within Christianity, we must place more emphasis on this interior dimension of Christianity, that is to say, on all that arises from the union of the soul with its God. The essential problem of Christianity in its present condition may well lie precisely in rediscovering that dimension of interiority, of the personal relationship of man to God, for it is this that constitutes an integral Christian existence. In the life of Christ there is his conversation with men and the way in which he puts himself at their service. But there is also that mysterious intimacy with his Father: "Christ went off into the hills to pray" (Mk. 6, 46), the gospel tells us. And the gospel is replete with these echoes of the intimacy of Christ with his Father: "My Father loves me, for I always do what pleases him . . . The Father and I are one" (Jn. 10, 30). We will have to struggle to maintain that dimension of interior life within ourselves; but without it all faith will in the end disappear.

I add that this encounter with God is also one of the elements on which our certitude of the truth of our faith is legitimately based. By that I mean that it is in the course of the spiritual journey of a person, from the first experiences of childhood or adolescence and the test of fidelity throughout a long life, that faith manifests itself as something so real that it would seem absurd to contest its authenticity. The experience of our encounter with God and of all that it gives us shows that it cannot be simply the expression of a passing illusion, of an enthusiasm or of an illuminism, but that it is a matter of a conviction whose solidity resists the hard experience of daily living with all the problems that it poses for us. From the religious point of view the nature of what is authentic is such as to be a permanent source of conversion: there are such fruits of authenticity about it that they constitute something undeniable. Paul expresses this in his letter to the Romans: "The Spirit himself and our spirit bear united witness that we are children of God" (8, 16). It has often been asked what this witness is that the Holy Spirit renders to our spirit, but this witness is the fruits that the knowledge of God and of Christ produces in our lives, and they are like something in whose presence we ourselves are astonished. In other words, the action of the Spirit in souls is so unquestionable that it testifies to its own reality. There is such a magnificent, such a fascinating presence of God in souls that it is surprising in this day and age that so many men disregard it. If this aspect had no foundation in faith, we might question ourselves as to its authenticity. But it comes in some way to confirm what justifies faith from the point of view of the intellect.

One conclusion can be drawn from all that we have said in this book. Ours is a world in which theoretical and practical atheism hold a large place. But we do not belong to the number of those who consider that this secularization and absence of God are inevitable. Personally, I positively am not conscious of having the vocation of some antediluvian monster, which one would call the religious animal and whose lost specimens could be placed in museums. If the religious man were the expression of the man of the past, he would not interest me in the least, for, after all, I belong to my time; what interests me is the humanity of my time and the humanity of tomorrow; what interests me is the growing youth. Now I maintain that this growing youth and this humanity of tomorrow will not set themselves up outside of God, but rather that God is called to occupy in the civilization of tomorrow the place he had in the civilization of the past; that atheism is the expression of a temporary crisis, but it is not at all clear that we have to resign ourselves to it. And it is all too evident that insofar as we do resign ourselves to it, play beaten in advance, and adopt defeatist attitudes, we render ourselves perfectly incapable of bringing God to a world that is seeking him perhaps far more than we think.

As I said before, the problem before us today is not simply a personal one. It is not simply the problem of our personal faith and of our personal interior life. It is a problem that is addressed to us even on the level of the city. We are conscious of a threat that affects us in the very core of what we believe. We sense this at all levels. We feel it on the level of the attacks from without, we feel it on the level of weaknesses from within, and that is why we feel the need to rediscover what constitutes the solid basis of our faith, what justifies our adherence to the content of the articles of our faith, what restores our desire for an interior life which so many obstacles make so difficult for us. The world around us is at this time in an ambiguous state; all political and ideological certitudes are shaken. But forces that seemed impressive to us are today becoming less threatening than we believed. There is a metaphysical anxiety that is in the process of being reborn in the heart of youth, and we see manifold expressions of it. In the presence of the enormous tasks which will be ours tomorrow, it is essential that the world find Christians who are prepared.

The essential problem today lies not in the forces that we have to confront from without. The danger is from within. The danger lies in allowing our faith, the institution, and interiority to become decomposed. The danger lies in disputes that would question the important articles of faith, from the virginal conception to the bodily resurrection of Christ. It lies in the basic issue of the ecclesial institution, of the authority and infallibility of the Sovereign Pontiff, of the value of the sacrament as constituting the vital milieu in which Christian experience grows. And when Christians, and even ecclesiatics, smile somewhat disdainfully when we speak of the Profession of Faith of Paul VI, this would scandalize us were it not a proof of infantilism. Where is the framework of the instruction we must give children, if not in Paul VI's profession of faith? I agree completely that it must be presented in a pedagogical way, but none of its content of faith, as reaffirmed by the Sovereign Pontiff, must be minimized. The essential responsibility today of the

Christian people is to see to it that the faith they have received, to which they are attached, preserves its full value. This Christian people also has the duty to grow stronger in this faith, to deepen it through a more solid religious knowledge, and to interiorize it through prayer. Only then can we banish all anxiety for the future. A future that will find a Christian people prepared will surely be able to extend itself in the direction of our hopes. We have the right to be optimistic, but to the extent that this optimism will be a fighting optimism. The future will not be given us by itself, but if we know how to contribute our share to it, we have no reason to believe that it will not be along the lines of a humanism in which God will have his rightful place and which will be able to raise up an authentically human civilization.